1

FOUR CORNERS

Second Edition

Student's Book
with Online Self-Study

JACK C. RICHARDS & DAVID BOHLKE

CAMBRIDGE
UNIVERSITY PRESS

CAMBRIDGE
UNIVERSITY PRESS

University Printing House, Cambridge CB2 8BS, United Kingdom

One Liberty Plaza, 20th Floor, New York, NY 10006, USA

477 Williamstown Road, Port Melbourne, VIC 3207, Australia

314–321, 3rd Floor, Plot 3, Splendor Forum, Jasola District Centre, New Delhi – 110025, India

79 Anson Road, #06–04/06, Singapore 079906

Cambridge University Press is part of the University of Cambridge.

It furthers the University's mission by disseminating knowledge in the pursuit of education, learning and research at the highest international levels of excellence.

www.cambridge.org
Information on this title: www.cambridge.org/fourcorners

© Cambridge University Press 2012, 2019

First published 2012
Second edition 2019

20 19 18 17 16 15 14 13 12 11 10 9 8 7

Printed in Poland by Opolgraf

A catalogue record for this publication is available from the British Library

ISBN 978-1-108-65961-1 Student's Book with Online Self-Study 1
ISBN 978-1-108-68741-6 Student's Book with Online Self-Study 1A
ISBN 978-1-108-64936-0 Student's Book with Online Self-Study 1B
ISBN 978-1-108-56045-0 Student's Book with Online Self-Study and Online Workbook 1
ISBN 978-1-108-56048-1 Student's Book with Online Self-Study and Online Workbook 1A
ISBN 978-1-108-56399-4 Student's Book with Online Self-Study and Online Workbook 1B
ISBN 978-1-108-45950-1 Workbook 1
ISBN 978-1-108-45953-2 Workbook 1A
ISBN 978-1-108-45955-6 Workbook 1B
ISBN 978-1-108-63367-3 Teacher's Edition with Complete Assessment Program 1
ISBN 978-1-108-64464-8 Full Contact with Online Self-Study 1
ISBN 978-1-108-59712-8 Full Contact with Online Self-Study 1A
ISBN 978-1-316-99950-9 Full Contact with Online Self-Study 1B
ISBN 978-1-108-45973-0 Presentation Plus Level 1

Additional resources for this publication at www.cambridge.org/fourcorners

Authors' acknowledgments

Many people contributed to the development of *Four Corners*. The authors and publisher would like to particularly thank the following **reviewers**:

Nele Noe, **Academy for Educational Development, Qatar Independent Secondary School for Girls**, Doha, Qatar; Pablo Stucchi, **Antonio Raimondi School** and **Instituto San Ignacio de Loyola**, Lima, Peru; Nadeen Katz, **Asia University**, Tokyo, Japan; Tim Vandenhoek, **Asia University**, Tokyo, Japan; Celso Frade and Sonia Maria Baccari de Godoy, **Associação Alumni**, São Paulo, Brazil; Rosane Bandeira, **Atlanta Idiomas**, Manaus, Brazil; Cacilda Reis da Silva, **Atlanta Idiomas**, Manaus, Brazil; Gretta Sicsu, **Atlanta Idiomas**, Manaus, Brazil; Naila Maria Cañiso Ferreira, **Atlanta Idiomas**, Manaus, Brazil; Hothnã Moraes de Souza Neto, **Atlanta Idiomas**, Manaus, Brazil; Jacqueline Kurtzious, **Atlanta Idiomas**, Manaus, Brazil; José Menezes Ribeiro Neto, **Atlanta Idiomas**, Manaus, Brazil; Sheila Ribeiro Cordeiro, **Atlanta Idiomas**, Manaus, Brazil; Juliana Fernandes, **Atlanta Idiomas**, Manaus, Brazil; Aline Alexandrina da Silva, **Atlanta Idiomas**, Manaus, Brazil; Kari Miller, **Binational Center**, Quito, Ecuador; Alex K. Oliveira, **Boston University**, Boston, MA, USA; Noriko Furuya, **Bunka Gakuen University**, Tokyo, Japan; Robert Hickling, **Bunka Gakuen University**, Tokyo, Japan; John D. Owen, **Bunka Gakuen University**, Tokyo, Japan; Elisabeth Blom, **Casa Thomas Jefferson**, Brasília, Brazil; Lucilena Oliveira Andrade, **Centro Cultural Brasil Estados Unidos (CCBEU Belém)**, Belém, Brazil; Marcelo Franco Borges, **Centro Cultural Brasil Estados Unidos (CCBEU Belém)**, Belém, Brazil; Geysa de Azevedo Moreira, **Centro Cultural Brasil Estados Unidos (CCBEU Belém)**, Belém, Brazil; Anderson Felipe Barbosa Negrão, **Centro Cultural Brasil Estados Unidos (CCBEU Belém)**, Belém, Brazil; Henry Grant, **CCBEU – Campinas**, Campinas, Brazil; Maria do Rosário, **CCBEU – Franca**, Franca, Brazil; Ane Cibele Palma, **CCBEU Inter Americano**, Curitiba, Brazil; Elen Flavia Penques da Costa, **Centro de Cultura Idiomas – Taubaté**, Taubaté, Brazil; Inara Lúcia Castillo Couto, **CEL LEP – São Paulo**, São Paulo, Brazil; Sonia Patricia Cardoso, **Centro de Idiomas Universidad Manuela Beltrán**, Barrio Cedritos, Colombia; Geraldine Itiago Losada, **Centro Universitario Grupo Sol (Musali)**, Mexico City, Mexico; Nick Hilmers, **DePaul University**, Chicago, IL, USA; Monica L. Montemayor Menchaca, **EDIMSA**, Metepec, Mexico; Angela Whitby, **Edu-Idiomas Language School**, Cholula, Puebla, Mexico; Mary Segovia, **El Monte Rosemead Adult School**, Rosemead, CA, USA; Dr. Deborah Aldred, **ELS Language Centers, Middle East Region**, Abu Dhabi, United Arab Emirates; Leslie Lott, **Embassy CES**, Ft. Lauderdale, FL, USA; M. Martha Lengeling, **Escuela de Idiomas**, Guanajuato, Mexico; Pablo Frias, **Escuela de Idiomas UNAPEC**, Santo Domingo, Dominican Republic; Tracy Vanderhoek, **ESL Language Center**, Toronto, Canada; Kris Vicca and Michael McCollister, **Feng Chia University**, Taichung, Taiwan; Flávia Patricia do Nascimento Martins, **First Idiomas**, Sorocaba, Brazil; Andrea Taylor, **Florida State University in Panama**, Panamá, Panama; Carlos Lizárraga González, **Grupo Educativo Angloamericano**, Mexico City, Mexico; Bo-Kyung Lee, **Hankuk University of Foreign Studies**, Seoul, South Korea; Dr. Martin Endley, **Hanyang University**, Seoul, South Korea; Mauro Luiz Pinheiro, **IBEU Ceará**, Ceará, Brazil; Ana Lúcia da Costa Maia de Almeida, **IBEU Copacabana**, Copacabana, Brazil; Maristela Silva, **ICBEU Manaus**, Manaus, Brazil; Magaly Mendes Lemos, **ICBEU São José dos Campos**, São José dos Campos, Brazil; Augusto Pelligrini Filho, **ICBEU São Luis**, São Luis, Brazil; Leonardo Mercado, **ICPNA**, Lima, Peru; Lucia Rangel Lugo, **Instituto Tecnológico de San Luis Potosí**, San Luis Potosí, Mexico; Maria Guadalupe Hernández Lozada, **Instituto Tecnológico de Tlalnepantla**, Tlalnepantla de Baz, Mexico; Karen Stewart, **International House Veracruz**, Veracruz, Mexico; Tom David, **Japan College of Foreign Languages**, Tokyo, Japan; Andy Burki, **Korea University, International Foreign Language School**, Seoul, South Korea; Jinseo Noh, **Kwangwoon University**, Seoul, South Korea; Neil Donachey, **La Salle Junior and Senior High School**, Kagoshima, Japan; Rich Hollingworth, **La Salle Junior and Senior High School**, Kagoshima, Japan; Quentin Kum, **La Salle Junior and Senior High School**, Kagoshima, Japan; Geoff Oliver, **La Salle Junior and Senior High School**, Kagoshima, Japan; Martin Williams, **La Salle Junior and Senior High School**, Kagoshima, Japan; Nadezhda Nazarenko, **Lone Star College**, Houston, TX, USA; Carolyn Ho, **Lone Star College-Cy-Fair**, Cypress, TX, USA; Kaoru Kuwajima, **Meijo University**, Nagoya, Japan; Alice Ya-fen Chou, **National Taiwan University of Science and Technology**, Taipei, Taiwan; Raymond Dreyer, **Northern Essex Community College**, Lawrence, MA, USA; Mary Keter Terzian Megale, **One Way Línguas-Suzano**, São Paulo, Brazil; B. Greg Dunne, **Osaka Shoin Women's University**, Higashi-Osaka, Japan; Robert Maran, **Osaka Shoin Women's University**, Higashi-Osaka, Japan; Bonnie Cheeseman, **Pasadena Community College** and **UCLA American Language Center**, Los Angeles, CA, USA; Simon Banha, **Phil Young's English School**, Curitiba, Brazil; Oh Jun Il, **Pukyong National University**, Busan, South Korea; Carmen Gehrke, **Quatrum English Schools**, Porto Alegre, Brazil; John Duplice, **Rikkyo University**, Tokyo, Japan; Wilzania da Silva Nascimento, **Senac**, Manaus, Brazil; Miva Silva Kingston, **Senac**, Manaus, Brazil; Lais Lima, **Senac**, Manaus, Brazil; Mengjiao Wu, **Shanghai Maritime University**, Shanghai, China; Wen hsiang Su, **Shih Chien University Kaohsiung Campus**, Kaohsiung, Taiwan; Yuan-hsun Chuang, **Soo Chow University**, Taipei, Taiwan; Lynne Kim, **Sun Moon University (Institute for Language Education)**, Cheon An City, Chung Nam, South Korea; Regina Ramalho, **Talken English School**, Curitiba, Brazil; Tatiana Mendonça, **Talken English School**, Curitiba, Brazil; Ricardo Todeschini, **Talken English School**, Curitiba, Brazil; Monica Carvalho da Rocha, **Talken English School**, Joinville, Brazil; Karina Schoene, **Talken English School**, Joinville, Brazil; Diaña Peña Munoz and Zira Kuri, **The Anglo**, Mexico City, Mexico; Christopher Modell, **Tokai University**, Tokyo, Japan; Song-won Kim, **TTI (Teacher's Training Institute)**, Seoul, South Korea; Nancy Alarcón, **UNAM FES Zaragoza Language Center**, Mexico City, Mexico; Laura Emilia Fierro López, **Universidad Autónoma de Baja California**, Mexicali, Mexico; María del Rocío Domínguez Gaona, **Universidad Autónoma de Baja California**, Tijuana, Mexico; Saul Santos Garcia, **Universidad Autónoma de Nayarit**, Nayarit, Mexico; Christian Meléndez, **Universidad Católica de El Salvador**, San Salvador, El Salvador; Irasema Mora Pablo, **Universidad de Guanajuato**, Guanajuato, Mexico; Alberto Peto, **Universidad de Oaxaca**, Tehuantepec, Mexico; Carolina Rodriguez Beltan, **Universidad Manuela Beltrán, Centro Colombo Americano**, and **Universidad Jorge Tadeo Lozano**, Bogotá, Colombia; Nidia Milena Molina Rodriguez, **Universidad Manuela Beltrán** and **Universidad Militar Nueva Granada**, Bogotá, Colombia; Yolima Perez Arias, **Universidad Nacional de Colombia**, Bogotá, Colombia; Héctor Vázquez García, **Universidad Nacional Autónoma de Mexico**, Mexico City, Mexico; Pilar Barrera, **Universidad Técnica de Ambato**, Ambato, Ecuador; Deborah Hulston, **University of Regina**, Regina, Canada; Rebecca J. Shelton, **Valparaiso University, Interlink Language Center**, Valparaiso, IN, USA; Tae Lee, **Yonsei University**, Seodaemun-gu, Seoul, South Korea; Claudia Thereza Nascimento Mendes, **York Language Institute**, Rio de Janeiro, Brazil; Jamila Jenny Hakam, **ELT Consultant**, Muscat, Oman; Stephanie Smith, **ELT Consultant**, Austin, TX, USA.

Scope and sequence

LEVEL 1	Learning outcomes	Grammar	Vocabulary
Welcome Unit Pages 2–3 **Classroom language** Page 4	**Students can ...** ☑ introduce themselves and others ☑ say hello and good-bye		
Unit 1 Pages 5–14			
New friends A *What's your name?* B *How do you spell it?* C *Are you a student?* D *Names and jobs*	**Students can ...** ☑ ask for and say names ☑ spell names ☑ talk about where people are from and what they do ☑ discuss people's names and jobs	The verb *be* Possessive adjectives Subject pronouns *Yes / no* questions with *be*	Names and titles Interesting jobs
Unit 2 Pages 15–24			
People and places A *Where are you from?* B *What's your email address?* C *Family* D *Family and friends*	**Students can ...** ☑ ask for and say people's nationalities ☑ ask for and give phone numbers and email addresses ☑ identify family members and give their ages ☑ give information about family and friends	Plural subject pronouns Questions with *be* *Who* and *How old* with *be*	Nationalities Family members Numbers 0–101
Unit 3 Pages 25–34			
What's that? A *Is this your notebook?* B *What's this called in English?* C *Clothing* D *Favorite things*	**Students can ...** ☑ ask about and identify everyday items ☑ ask what something is called in English ☑ talk about clothes and possessions ☑ describe favorite possessions	Demonstratives Articles *a* and *an* Plurals Possessive pronouns *Whose* *'s* and *s'*	Everyday items Clothes and colors
Unit 4 Pages 35–44			
Daily life A *Getting around* B *What time is it?* C *My routine* D *My weekend*	**Students can ...** ☑ describe how people get around ☑ ask for and tell the time ☑ ask and answer questions about routines ☑ describe the things they do on weekends	Simple present statements Simple present *yes / no* questions	Ways of getting around Days of the week and routines
Unit 5 Pages 45–54			
Free time A *Online habits* B *How much is it?* C *What do you do for fun?* D *Online fun*	**Students can ...** ☑ talk about their online habits ☑ accept and decline help ☑ ask and answer questions about leisure activities ☑ discuss how they use technology	Adverbs of frequency Simple present *Wh-* questions with do	Online activities Leisure activities and places
Unit 6 Pages 55–64			
Work and play A *What does she do?* B *Can I speak to ... ?* C *Can you sing?* D *Work and study*	**Students can ...** ☑ identify and talk about jobs ☑ ask for someone on the telephone ☑ have someone wait ☑ describe their talents and abilities ☑ talk about study and work programs	Simple present *Wh-* questions with *does* *Can* for ability *And, but,* and *or*	Jobs Abilities

Functional language	Listening and Pronunciation	Reading and Writing	Speaking
Interactions: Saying hello Saying good-bye			• Introductions • Greetings
Interactions: Asking for spelling	**Listening:** Spelling names **Pronunciation:** Contractions	**Reading:** "Famous Names" An article **Writing:** My name	• Class introductions and greetings • *Keep talking*: Name circle • Class name list • Guessing game about famous people • *Keep talking*: "Find the differences" activity about jobs and cities • Quiz about celebrities
Interactions: Asking for someone's phone number Asking for someone's email address	**Listening:** Directory Assistance calls Information forms People I know **Pronunciation:** Word stress	**Reading:** "People in My Life" Photo captions **Writing:** My friends	• True and false information about people • *Keep talking*: Interviews with new identities • Class survey for new contact information • Information exchange about family members • *Keep talking*: Family trees • Presentation about friends
Interactions: Asking what something is	**Listening:** Things around the classroom Favorite things **Pronunciation:** Plurals	**Reading:** "Yuna's Blog: My favorite things!" A blog post **Writing:** My favorite thing	• Questions and answers about personal items • *Keep talking*: Things in the closet • Memory game about everyday items • Personal items and their owners • *Keep talking*: "Find the differences" activity about clothing colors • Presentation of favorite things
Interactions: Asking the time	**Listening:** Times of different events Angela's routine **Pronunciation:** Reduction of *to*	**Reading:** "What's your favorite day of the week?" A message board **Writing:** About my weekend	• Survey about getting to school and work • *Keep talking*: Transportation facts • Interview about the times of specific events • Interview about routines • *Keep talking*: "Find someone who" activities about routines • Survey about busy weekends
Interactions: Declining help Accepting help	**Listening:** Shopping Favorite websites **Pronunciation:** Thirteen or thirty?	**Reading:** "Fun Online Activities" An article **Writing:** Let's chat	• Comparison of online habits • *Keep talking*: Interview about online habits • Role play of a shopping situation • Interview about leisure activities • *Keep talking*: Interviews about fun activities • Discussion about favorite websites
Interactions: Asking for someone on the phone Having someone wait	**Listening:** Telephone calls Ads for overseas programs **Pronunciation:** *Can* and *can't*	**Reading:** "Fun Jobs" An article **Writing:** My abilities	• "Find someone who" activity about jobs • *Keep talking*: Memory game about jobs • Role play of a phone call • Interview about abilities • *Keep talking*: Board game about abilities • Discussion about study and work programs

LEVEL 1	Learning outcomes	Grammar	Vocabulary
Unit 7 Pages 65–74			
Food A *Breakfast, lunch, and dinner* B *I like Chinese food!* C *Meals* D *Favorite food*	**Students can ...** ☑ say what meals they eat ☑ say what they like and dislike ☑ talk about their eating habits ☑ talk about their favorite food	Count and noncount nouns *Some* and *any* *How often* Time expressions	Food More food
Unit 8 Pages 75–84			
In the neighborhood A *Around town* B *How do I get to ... ?* C *Fun in the city* D *A great place to visit*	**Students can ...** ☑ give the locations of neighborhood places ☑ ask for and give directions ☑ talk about interesting places in their towns ☑ give a presentation on a city attraction	Prepositions of location *There is, there are*	Places in the neighborhood Places to visit
Unit 9 Pages 85–94			
What are you doing? A *I'm looking for you.* B *I can't talk right now.* C *These days* D *What's new?*	**Students can ...** ☑ describe what people are doing right now ☑ ask if someone can talk right now ☑ explain why they can't talk on the telephone ☑ describe what people are doing these days ☑ discuss what people are doing	Present continuous statements Present continuous questions	Actions and prepositions Activities
Unit 10 Pages 95–104			
Past experiences A *Last weekend* B *You're kidding!* C *Did you make dinner last night?* D *I saw a great movie.*	**Students can ...** ☑ say what they did last weekend ☑ show that they're listening ☑ express surprise ☑ talk about routine events in the past ☑ talk about past activities	Simple past regular verbs Simple past irregular verbs *Yes / no* questions	Weekend activities Things to do
Unit 11 Pages 105–114			
Getting away A *Where were you?* B *That's great!* C *My vacation* D *Travel experiences*	**Students can ...** ☑ describe where they were in the past ☑ react to news ☑ talk about their last vacation ☑ describe a vacation	Past of *be* Simple past *Wh-* questions	Adjectives Vacation activities
Unit 12 Pages 115–124			
Time to celebrate A *I'm going to get married.* B *Sure. I'd love to.* C *Planning a party* D *Birthdays*	**Students can ...** ☑ talk about their plans for specific dates ☑ accept or decline an invitation ☑ discuss and agree on plans ☑ describe birthday traditions in their culture	*Be going to* *Yes / no* questions *Wh-* questions with *be going to* Object pronouns	Months and dates Party checklist

Functional language	Listening and Pronunciation	Reading and Writing	Speaking
Interactions: Expressing dislikes Expressing likes	**Listening:** Food preferences A typical Swedish meal **Pronunciation:** Word Stress	**Reading:** "My Favorite Food" An article **Writing:** A typical meal	• Survey about meals • *Keep talking*: Recipes • Information exchange about food preferences • Comparison of eating habits • *Keep talking*: Discussion about eating habits • Interview about favorite food
Interactions: Asking for directions	**Listening:** GPS directions Tourist information **Pronunciation:** Word stress	**Reading:** "Escape Rooms" A magazine article **Writing:** Group poster	• Information exchange with maps • *Keep talking*: Information gap activity with neighborhood maps • Role play about directions • Interview about places in town • *Keep talking*: Description of an unusual zoo • Presentation about a city attraction
Interactions: Asking if someone can talk now Explaining that you can't talk now	**Listening:** Sound effects Telephone calls **Pronunciation:** Intonation in questions	**Reading:** "Status Updates" A micro-blog **Writing:** My status update	• Guessing game about people's actions • *Keep talking*: Interpretations of actions • Role play of a phone call • "Find someone who" activity about things people are doing these days • *Keep talking*: Guessing game about who's doing what • Speculations about someone's activities
Interactions: Showing that you're listening Expressing surprise	**Listening:** Diana's week Matt's busy week **Pronunciation:** Simple past *-ed* endings	**Reading:** "Matt's Movie Reviews" Blog post **Writing:** A blog post	• Information exchange about last weekend • *Keep talking*: Picture story • Role play of surprising conversations • Interview about routine events in the past • *Keep talking*: Memories • "Find someone who" activity about past activities
Interactions: Reacting to good news Reacting to bad news	**Listening:** A short trip Three vacations **Pronunciation:** Reduction of *did you*	**Reading:** "Travel Tales" Blog posts **Writing:** A postcard	• Interview about where you were • *Keep talking*: Interview about school trips • Class exchange of personal news • Information exchange about vacations • *Keep talking*: Speculation about a vacation • Presentation of postcards
Interactions: Declining an invitation Accepting an invitation	**Listening:** Invitations A "Sweet 16" birthday party **Pronunciation:** Reduction of *going to*	**Reading:** "Birthday Traditions" An article **Writing:** A thank-you note	• Information exchange about special days • *Keep talking*: Weekend plans • Class invitations • Discussion of plans for three scenarios • *Keep talking*: Plan for a party • Discussion about birthday traditions

Welcome

1 Introducing yourself

A 🎧 Listen and practice.

> **Simon** Hello. I'm Simon.
> **Chen** Hi, Simon. My name is Chen. Nice to meet you.
> **Simon** Nice to meet you, too.

B `PAIR WORK` Introduce yourselves.

2 Introducing someone else

A 🎧 Listen and practice.

> **Simon** Chen, this is my friend Sofia.
> **Sofia** Hi, Chen. Nice to meet you.
> **Chen** Nice to meet you, too, Sofia.

B `GROUP WORK` Introduce your partner from Exercise 1 to another classmate.

3 Hi and bye

A 🎧 Listen and practice.

Simon Hi, Chen!
 Chen Good morning, Simon! How are you?
Simon I'm fine, thanks. And you?
 Chen Fine, thank you.

Simon See you later, Chen!
 Chen Bye, Simon!

B 🎧 Listen to the expressions. Then practice the conversation again with the new expressions.

Saying hello
Hi.
Hello.
Good morning.
Good afternoon.
Good evening.

Saying good-bye
Bye.
Good-bye.
See you.
See you later.
See you tomorrow.

C CLASS ACTIVITY Say hello to your classmates and ask how they are. Then say good-bye.

I can introduce myself and others. ✓
I can say hello and good-bye. ✓

3

Classroom language 🎧

Pair work

Group work

Class activity

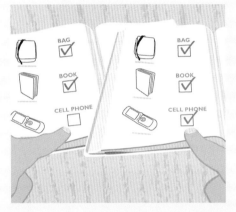

Compare answers.

Cover the picture.

Go to page 12.

Ask and answer questions.

Interview your partner.

Role-play the situation.

1 New friends

LESSON A	**LESSON B**	**LESSON C**	**LESSON D**
● Names and titles ● The verb *be*; possessive adjectives	● Asking for spelling	● Interesting jobs ● Subject pronouns; *yes* / *no* questions with *be*	● Reading: "Famous Names" ● Writing: My name

1. Noah

2. Liam

3. William

4. Mason

5. James

1. Emma

2. Olivia

3. Ava

4. Sophia

5. Isabella

Noah

Sophia

Michael

James

Harper

Warm Up

Popular names in the United States

A Check (✓) the popular names.

B Say ten popular names in your country.

A What's your name?

1 Language in context First day of class

🎧 Listen to Ms. Peters meet her students on the first day of class. <u>Underline</u> the names.

> Hello, everyone. I'm your teacher, <u>Ms. Peters</u>. My first name is Linda.

> Hi. What's your name?

> My name is Maria Gomez.

> Hi. I'm Maria. What are your names?

> My name is Ricardo.

> And I'm Yoko. Nice to meet you.

> What are their names?

> Her name is Yoko. His name is Ricardo.

2 Vocabulary Names and titles

A 🎧 Listen and repeat.

first name   middle name   last / family name

Jennifer Ann Wilson
full name

Miss Gomez = a single woman

Mrs. Chow = a married woman

Ms. Peters = a single or married woman

Mr. Adams = a single or married man

B PAIR WORK Complete the sentences with your own information. Then compare answers.

My first name is _____ .   My full name is _____ .

My family name is _____ .   My teacher's name is _____ .

3 Grammar 🎧 The verb *be*; possessive adjectives

What is (What's)	your name?	**My** name **is** Maria.
	his name?	**His** name **is** Ricardo.
	her name?	**Her** name **is** Yoko.
What are	your names?	**Our** names **are** Maria and Jason.
	their names?	**Their** names **are** Ricardo and Yoko.

A Circle the correct words. Then compare with a partner.

1 Maria is a student. **His** /**Her** last name is Gomez.

2 Ms. Peters **is** / **are** our teacher. **Her** / **Their** first name is Linda.

3 My name is Jason. What's **our** / **your** name?

4 Anna and Bruce **is** / **are** students. **Her** / **Their** teacher is Miss Brown.

5 Their first names **is** / **are** Yoko and Ricardo.

6 Hello, everyone. I'm Miss Diaz. What are **your** / **his** names?

B Complete the conversation with the correct words. Then practice in a group.

A Hello. Welcome to English class. What ___is___ your name, please?

B _____ name is Pam.

A And what's _____ last name, Pam?

B My last name _____ Nelson.

A OK. And _____ is *your* name?

C Ji-ah. _____ family name is Lee.

4 Speaking My name is ...

A **CLASS ACTIVITY** Meet your classmates. Say your first and last name.

A: Hello. My name is Oscar Martinez. What's your name?

B: Hi. My name is Susana Harris.

A: It's nice to meet you.

B: Nice to meet you, too.

B Share your information.

A: What's his name?

B: His name is Oscar Martinez. What's her name?

A: Sorry, I don't know.

5 Keep talking!

Go to page 125 for more practice.

I can ask for and say names. ✓

B How do you spell it?

1 The alphabet

A 🎧 Listen and repeat.

A	B	C	D	E	F	G	H	I	J	K	L	M

N	O	P	Q	R	S	T	U	V	W	X	Y	Z

B `PAIR WORK` Say a letter. Your partner points to it. Take turns.

2 Interactions Spelling names

A 🎧 Listen and practice.

Donald Hello. My name is Donald Wang.

Clerk How do you spell your first name?

Donald D-O-N-A-L-D.

Clerk And how do you spell your last name?

Donald W-A-N-G.

Asking for spelling

> How do you spell your first name?　　　> How do you spell your last name?

B `PAIR WORK` Practice the conversation again with these names.

John Evans	Cindy Douglas	Antonia Lopez	Richard Wu

A: Hello. My name is John Evans.

B: Hello, John. How do you spell your first name?

A: J-O-H-N.

B: And how do you spell . . . ?

3 Listening Spell it!

A 🎧 Listen to four people spell their names. Check (✓) the correct answers.

1 ☑ Steven   2 ☐ Dina   3 ☐ Kelly   4 ☐ Bryan
  ☐ Stephen   ☐ Dena   ☐ Kerry   ☐ Brian

B 🎧 Listen to the conversations. Write the names.

HELLO.
My name is

George _____ .

1

CITY COLLEGE
STUDENT ID

_____ Watkins

2

10:00 English Class

1. _____ _____

3

24 HOUR GYM

Mr.   (Miss)   Mrs.

First name _____

Last name _____

4

First name: Paul
Middle name:
Last name:

5

Welcome, students!
Ms. _____

6

4 Speaking A class list

CLASS ACTIVITY Ask your classmates for their names. Make a list.

A: What's your first name?
B: Tyler.
A: How do you spell it?
B: T-Y-L-E-R.
A: And what's your last name?
B: Larsen.

First names	Last names
Tyler	Larsen
Lindsey	Fisher
Marcela	Perez
Evan	Howley
Dmitri	Benos

I can spell names. ✓

C Are you a student?

1 Vocabulary Interesting jobs

A 🎧 Listen and repeat.

Salma Hayek is an **actress**.
She's from Mexico.

Tadanobu Asano is an **actor**.
He's from Japan.

Alex Hornest is an **artist**.
He's from Brazil.

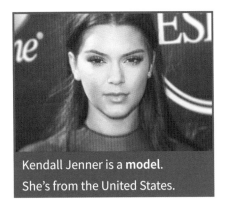
Kendall Jenner is a **model**.
She's from the United States.

Lang Lang is a **musician**.
He's from China.

Rihanna is a **singer**.
She's from Barbados.

B **PAIR WORK** Name other people for each job.

A: Jet Li is an actor.

B: Yes. And Meryl Streep is an actress.

2 Conversation My friend the musician

🎧 Listen and practice.

Sandy	Hey, Jacob!
Jacob	Oh, hi, Sandy. How's it going?
Sandy	Good, thanks. This is my friend Kevin.
Jacob	Hi. Nice to meet you.
Kevin	Nice to meet you, Jacob.
Jacob	Are you a student here?
Kevin	No, I'm not. I'm a musician.
Sandy	Kevin is from England.
Jacob	Oh? Are you from London?
Kevin	No, I'm not. I'm from Liverpool.

3 Grammar 🎧 Subject pronouns; *yes* / *no* questions with *be*

I'm a musician.	**Am I** in your class? Yes, **you are**. No, **you're not**. / No, **you aren't**.
You're a student.	**Are you** from London? Yes, **I am**. No, **I'm not**.
Kevin **is** from Liverpool. **He's** from Liverpool.	**Is he** a singer? Yes, **he is**. No, **he's not**. / No, **he isn't**.
Sandy **is** a student. **She's** a student.	**Is she** from Canada? Yes, **she is**. No, **she's not**. / No, **she isn't**.
Liverpool **is** in England. **It's** in England.	**Is your** name John? Yes, **it is**. No, **it's not**. / No, **it isn't**.

Contractions I'm = I am   you're = you are   he's = he is   she's = she is   it's = it is

A Match the questions and the answers. Then practice with a partner.

1 Is your first name Jacob? ___d___
2 Are you from Liverpool? _____
3 Is she from the United States? _____
4 Is she a musician? _____
5 Is Will Smith an actor? _____
6 Is Quito in Peru? _____

a No, I'm not. I'm from London.
b Yes, he is. He's a singer, too.
c No, she's not. She's an artist.
d Yes, it is. And my last name is King.
e No, it's not. It's in Ecuador.
f Yes, she is. She's from California.

B Complete the conversations with the correct words. Then practice with a partner.

1 A ___Is___ your first name Don?
  B No, _____ not. It's Jeff.

2 A _____ you from Mexico?
  B Yes, I _____ . I'm from Mexico City.

3 A _____ your teacher from England?
  B No, she _____ .

4 A _____ you a model?
  B No, _____ not. I'm a singer.

4 Pronunciation Contractions

🎧 **Listen and repeat. Notice the reduction of contractions.**

I am → I'm   he is → he's   it is → it's   are not → aren't

you are → you're   she is → she's   is not → isn't

5 Speaking Ten questions

GROUP WORK Think of a famous person with a job from Exercise 1. Your group
asks ten questions and guesses the name. Take turns.

A: Is the person a man?
B: No, she's not.
C: Is she an actress?

6 Keep talking!

Student A go to page 126 and Student B go to page 128 for more practice.

I can talk about where people are from and what they do. ✓

D Names and Jobs

1 Reading 🎧

A Look at the pictures. What are their names?

B Read the article. Are they all singers?

FAMOUS NAMES

Actor **Tom Cruise** uses his middle name as his last name. His full name is Thomas Cruise Mapother. Tom is short for Thomas.

Zhang Ziyi is an actress from China. Zhang isn't her first name. It's her family name. In China, family names come first.

Shakira is a singer from Colombia. She uses only her first name. Her full name is Shakira Isabel Mebarak Ripoll.

Jay-Z is a hip-hop singer from the United States. Jay-Z is his nickname. His real name is Shawn Corey Carter.

Pelé is a soccer player from Brazil. His full name is Edson Arantes do Nascimento. Pelé is his nickname.

Madonna is not a nickname for this singer. It's her first name. Her full name is Madonna Louise Veronica Ciccone.

C Read the article again. Complete the sentences with the correct words.

1 Tom Cruise uses his ____middle____ name as his last name.

2 Shakira uses only her _____ name.

3 Edson Arantes do Nascimento's _____ is Pelé.

4 Ziyi is not Zhang Ziyi's _____ name.

5 Jay-Z's _____ name is Shawn Corey Carter.

6 Madonna Louise Veronica Ciccone is Madonna's _____ name.

D PAIR WORK Tell your partner about another famous person's name.

"Rain is a singer, actor, and model from South Korea. Rain is his nickname. His real name is Jeong Ji-hoon."

2 **Writing** My name

A Write sentences about your name. Use the model to help you.

> **My Name**
>
> My full name is Anthony Steven Johnson.
> My nickname is Big Tony. Tony is short for
> Anthony. My middle name is Steven, and
> my last name is Johnson.

B GROUP WORK Tell your group about your name.

3 **Speaking** Celebrity quiz

A PAIR WORK Ask and answer the questions about celebrities.

1 She's an actress from the U.K. Her initials are E. W. What's her name?

   "Her name is Emma Watson."

2 She's an actress from Colombia. Her last name is Vergara. What's her first name?

3 He's a soccer player from Argentina. His first name is Lionel. What's his last name?

4 She's an actress and singer. Her nickname is J-Lo. What's her name?

5 He's an actor from Australia. His first name is Hugh. What's his last name?

6 She's an actress from the United States. Her last name is Lawrence. What's her first name?

B PAIR WORK Create a quiz. Write three sentences about a celebrity.

He's a basketball player.
He's from the United States.
His first name is LeBron.

C GROUP WORK Say your sentences to another pair. They guess the celebrity. Take turns.

A: He's a soccer player.
B: Is he Neymar?
A: No, he isn't. He's from Portugal.

I can discuss people's names and jobs. ✓

Wrap-up

1 Quick pair review

Lesson A Do you remember?

What are your classmates' last names? Answer with the information you remember.
You have two minutes.

A: Her last name is Fernandes.

B: Yes, it is. And his first name is Oscar. What's his last name?

A: It's Medina.

Lesson B Test your partner!

Say your full name. Can your partner write it correctly? Check his or her answer.
You have two minutes.

First name	Middle name	Last / Family name

Lesson C Brainstorm!

Make a list of interesting jobs. How many do you know? You have one minute.

Lesson D Guess!

Describe your favorite celebrity, but don't say his or her name! Can your partner
guess the name? Take turns. You have two minutes.

A: He's a singer and a musician. He's from the United States. He's in Maroon 5.

B: Is he Adam Levine?

A: Yes!

2 In the real world

What is your favorite movie? Go online and find information in English about
five actors or actresses in the movie. Then write about them.

- What are their names?
- Where are they from?

Actors in "The Avengers"

My favorite movie is "The Avengers."
Chris Hemsworth is an actor in the movie.
He's from Australia …

2 People and places

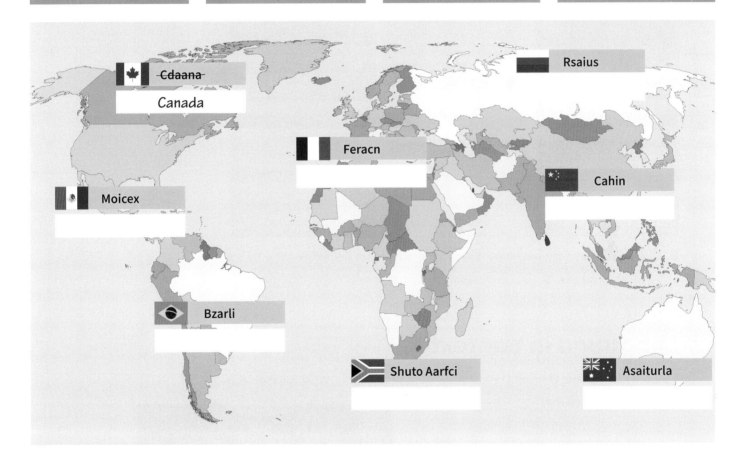

Canada ~~Cdaana~~ Canada
Rsaius
Feracn
Cahin
Moicex
Bzarli
Shuto Aarfci
Asaiturla

Warm Up

A Write the names of the countries.

B Say the names of five other countries in English.

A Where are you from?

1 Vocabulary Nationalities

A 🎧 Complete the chart with the correct nationalities. Then listen and check your answers.

Mexican	American	South Korean	Chilean	Greek	Colombian
Spanish	Canadian	Brazilian	Saudi	Peruvian	Japanese
British	Chinese	Turkish	Thai	Ecuadorian	✓ Australian

Country		Nationality	Country		Nationality
	Australia	Australian		Japan	
	Brazil			Mexico	
	Britain			Peru	
	Canada			Saudi Arabia	
	Chile			South Korea	
	China			Spain	
	Colombia			Thailand	
	Ecuador			Turkey	
	Greece			The United States	

B **PAIR WORK** Say a famous name. Your partner says his or her nationality. Take turns.

A: Mark Zuckerberg.

B: He's from the United States. He's American.

2 Language in context New neighbors

🎧 Listen to Brad and Emily Hill talk about their new neighbors. What are their names?

Brad	Who are they?
Emily	Oh, they're our new neighbors, Carlos and Claudia.
Brad	Are they musicians?
Emily	Yes, they are.
Brad	Where are they from?
Emily	They're from Brazil.
Brad	What city are they from?
Emily	They're from Manaus.

3 Grammar 🎧 Plural subject pronouns; questions with *be*

Where are you and Sakura from?	**Where** are Carlos and Claudia from?
We're from Japan.	**They're** from Brazil.
What city are **you** from?	**What** city are **they** from?
We're from Osaka.	**They're** from Manaus.
Are you Japanese?	**Are they** Brazilian?
Yes, **we are.**	Yes, **they are.**
No, **we're not.** / No, **we aren't.**	No, **they're not.** / No, **they aren't.**

Contractions   we're = we are   they're = they are

Complete the conversations with the correct words. Then practice with a partner.

1 A Where are _____ you _____ from?

   B We're from Mexico.

   A Oh? _____ city are you from? Are you from Mexico City?

   B No, we _____ not. _____ from Monterrey.

2 A _____ Jim and Carly American?

   B No, they _____ . They _____ Canadian.

   A What city in Canada are _____ from?

   B They _____ from Toronto.

4 Pronunciation Word stress

A 🎧 **Listen and repeat. Notice the stressed syllables in the nationalities.**

●	●•	•●•	•●
Greek	**Brit**ish	Bra**zil**ian	Chi**nese**

B 🎧 **Listen and repeat. Underline the stressed syllables in the nationalities.**

Japa<u>nese</u>   Australian   Spanish   Thai

5 Speaking That's not correct!

A Write three false sentences about people, countries, or nationalities.

   1. Rio de Janeiro and São Paulo are in Portugal.

   2. Beyoncé and Solange are British.

   3. Kate and Pippa Middleton are Australian.

B **GROUP WORK** **Share your sentences. Your group corrects them. Take turns.**

   A: Rio de Janeiro and São Paulo are in Portugal.

   B: No, they aren't. They're in Brazil.

6 Keep talking!

Go to page 127 for more practice.

I can ask for and say people's nationalities. ✓

B What's your email address?

1 Numbers 0 to 10; phone numbers; email addresses

A 🎧 Listen and repeat.

0	1	2	3	4	5	6	7	8	9	10
zero	one	two	three	four	five	six	seven	eight	nine	ten

B 🎧 Listen and repeat. Notice that people sometimes say "oh" for "zero" in phone numbers.

281-363-2301 = "two-eight-one, three-six-three, two-three-zero-one"

602-374-4188 = "six-oh-two, three-seven-four, four-one-eight-eight"

C 🎧 Listen and repeat. Notice the way people say email addresses.

susan8k@cup.org = "susan-eight-K-at-C-U-P-dot-org"

jun_akita@email.com = "jun-underscore-akita-at-email-dot-com"

2 Interactions Phone numbers and email addresses

A 🎧 Listen and practice.

Stacy	Hey, Emma. What's your phone number?
Emma	It's 309-403-8708.
Stacy	What's your email address?
Emma	It's emma@cup.org.
Stacy	Thanks!

B 🎧 Listen to the expressions. Then practice the conversation again with the new expressions.

Asking for someone's phone number

What's your phone number?   What's your number?

Asking for someone's email address

What's your email address?   What's your email?

C **PAIR WORK** Practice the conversation again with the information below.

978-887-8045   ej5@cup.org

604-608-4864   emma_jones@email.com

3 Listening What name, please?

A 🎧 Listen to four people call Directory Assistance for phone numbers.
Check (✓) the correct answers.

1 Carlos Moreno ☐ 333-822-1607 ✓ 323-822-1607
2 Lucy Chang ☐ 662-651-0410 ☐ 662-615-0410
3 Michael Ashcroft ☐ 866-279-9400 ☐ 866-279-9500
4 Beatriz J. Lago ☐ 341-360-7450 ☐ 341-360-4570

B 🎧 Listen to three people give their names, phone numbers, and email addresses.
Complete the forms.

MADISON ENGLISH SCHOOL

REGISTRATION

First name: _Michael_
Middle name: _John_
Last name: _____
Phone: _____
Email: _____

1-2-3 GYM

MEMBERSHIP

First name: _____
Middle initial: _P._
Last name: _____
Phone: _____
Email: _____

CityLibrary

CARD APPLICATION

First name: _____
Family name: _____
City: _Dallas_
Phone: _____
Email: _____

4 Speaking A new number and email address

A Write a new phone number and email address.

My new phone number: _____ My new email address: _____

B **CLASS ACTIVITY** Ask five classmates for their names, new phone numbers, and
new email addresses. Complete the chart with their answers.

	Name	Phone number	Email address
1			
2			
3			
4			
5			

C Share your information.

A: What's her name and phone number?

B: Her name is Fatima. Her phone number is 212-691-3239.

A: What's her email address?

B: Her email is …

I can ask for and give phone numbers and email addresses. ✓

C Family

1 Vocabulary Family members

A 🎧 Listen and repeat.

- grandparents
- grandfather Roger Mills
- grandmother Sarah Mills
- parents
- father (dad) Michael Olson
- mother (mom) Helen Olson
- children / kids
- husband
- wife
- daughter
- son
- sister Wendy Olson
- brother Jack Olson
- brother Brian Olson

B **PAIR WORK** Ask and answer the questions about the family in Part A.

1 Are Sarah and Roger Mills single?

2 Are Michael and Helen brother and sister?

3 Are Sarah and Roger grandparents?

4 Are Wendy and Jack parents?

2 Conversation Who's that?

🎧 Listen and practice.

Lance Who's that?

Jack That's my sister. Her name is Wendy.

Lance How old is she?

Jack She's seven.

Lance Is she your only sister?

Jack Yeah.

Lance And who are they?

Jack They're my grandparents.

Lance Wow. They look young.
And who's he?

Jack That's me!

3 Grammar 🎧 *Who* and *How Old* with *be*

Who's that?
    That's my sister.
How old is she?
    She's seven (years old).
	Who are they?
	    They're my grandparents.
	How old are they?
	    They're 70 and 66.

A Read the answers. Write the questions. Then practice with a partner.

A   Who's that?

B   Oh, that's my brother Ignacio.

A   _____

B   He's ten years old.

A   _____

B   They're my sisters Lucia, Antonia, and Carmen.

A   _____

B   They're 19, 16, and 11.

A   And _____

B   That's my grandfather.

A   _____

B   He's 62.

B **PAIR WORK** Ask and answer questions about the family in Exercise 1.

A: Who's that?

B: That's Jack Olson.

4 Speaking My family

A Complete the chart with information about three people in your family.

	Family member	Name	How old ... ?	Where ... from?
1				
2				
3				

B **PAIR WORK** Tell your partner about your family. Ask and answer questions for more information.

A: Keiko is my grandmother. She's 73.

B: Where is she from?

5 Keep talking!

Go to page 129 for more practice.

🎧 **Numbers 11-101**

11 eleven
12 twelve
13 thirteen
14 fourteen
15 fifteen
16 sixteen
17 seventeen
18 eighteen
19 nineteen
20 twenty
21 twenty-one
22 twenty-two
23 twenty-three
24 twenty-four
25 twenty-five
26 twenty-six
27 twenty-seven
28 twenty-eight
29 twenty-nine
30 thirty
40 forty
50 fifty
60 sixty
70 seventy
80 eighty
90 ninety
100 one hundred
101 one hundred (and) one

I can identify family members and give their ages. ✓

D Family and friends

1 Reading 🎧

A Look at the people in Isabel's photos. Who are they? Guess.

B Read the photo descriptions. Who are Isabel's family members? Who are her friends?

PEOPLE IN MY LIFE

I'm with my friends Fernando and Amy. Fernando is on the left. He's from Bogotá, Colombia. Amy is on the right. She's from Perth, Australia. I'm in the middle.

This is my brother Carlos and my sister Julia. Carlos is 18 years old and a good soccer player. Julia is only ten. She's a good tennis player.

This is my grandmother. Her name is Olivia, but her nickname is Nana. She's an artist, and she's 92 years old!

Here's my Internet friend Dong-sun. His family name is Choi. He's from Busan, South Korea. He's 18 years old. His sister is in the photo, too.

C Read the photo descriptions again. Correct the false sentences.

1 Isabel and Amy are ~~sisters~~.   Isabel and Amy are friends.

2 Carlos isn't a good soccer player.   _____

3 Olivia is 90 years old.   _____

4 Isabel and Dong-sun are classmates.   _____

D PAIR WORK Ask and answer the questions about Isabel's family and friends.

- Who are Fernando and Amy?
- What's Olivia's nickname?
- How old is Julia?
- What city is Dong-sun from?

2 Listening People I know

A 🎧 Listen to Gina show some photos to her friend. Who are the people?
Check (✓) the correct answers.

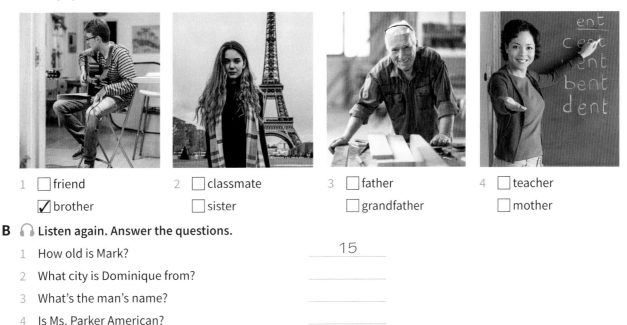

1 ☐ friend
  ☑ brother

2 ☐ classmate
  ☐ sister

3 ☐ father
  ☐ grandfather

4 ☐ teacher
  ☐ mother

B 🎧 Listen again. Answer the questions.

1 How old is Mark? _____15_____

2 What city is Dominique from? _____

3 What's the man's name? _____

4 Is Ms. Parker American? _____

3 Writing and speaking My friends

A Complete the chart with information about three friends. Then find photos or
draw pictures of them.

	Friend 1	Friend 2	Friend 3
Name			
Age			
Nationality			
Other information			

B Write sentences about your friends in the pictures. Use the
model and your answers in Part A to help you.

My friends

My best friend is Samantha. She's 26 years old.

She's American. She's a teacher.

Emma is my friend, too. She's ...

C **GROUP WORK** Share your pictures and sentences. Ask and answer questions
for more information.

A: This is my friend Samantha. She's 26 years old.

B: What's her last name?

I can give information about family and friends. ✓

Wrap-up

1 Quick pair review

Lesson A Guess!
Say five countries. Can your partner name the nationalities? Take turns.
You have two minutes.

A: South Korea.

B: South Korean.

Lesson B Test your partner!
Write three phone numbers and say them to your partner. Can your partner
write them correctly? Check his or her answers. You have two minutes.

My phone numbers	My partner's phone numbers

Lesson C Brainstorm!
Make a list of family words. How many do you know? You have one minute.

Lesson D Find out!
Are any of your friends or family members from the same cities? You have
two minutes.

A: My father is from Mexico City, and my mother is from Guadalajara.

B: My grandmother is from Guadalajara, too!

2 In the real world

Go online and find information in English about a country from another part
of the world. Then write about it.

- What are five cities in the country?
- What are the names and ages of two famous people
  from the country?

Busan

South Korean Cities and People
Seoul, Busan, Incheon, Daegu, and Ulsan are five
cities in South Korea. Daniel Dae Kim is a famous
actor from Busan, South Korea. He's …

3 What's that?

LESSON A
- Everyday items
- Demonstratives; articles *a* and *an*; plurals

LESSON B
- Asking what something is

LESSON C
- Clothes and colors
- Possessive pronouns; *Whose*; *'s* and *s'*

LESSON D
- Reading: "Yuna's Blog: My favorite things!"
- Writing: My favorite thing

Year: _____ 1969 _____

Year: _____

Year: _____

Year: _____

Warm Up

A Label the pictures with the correct years.

✓ 1969	1995	1978	1986

B Can you name five things in the pictures?

A Is this your notebook?

1 Vocabulary Everyday items

A 🎧 Listen and repeat.

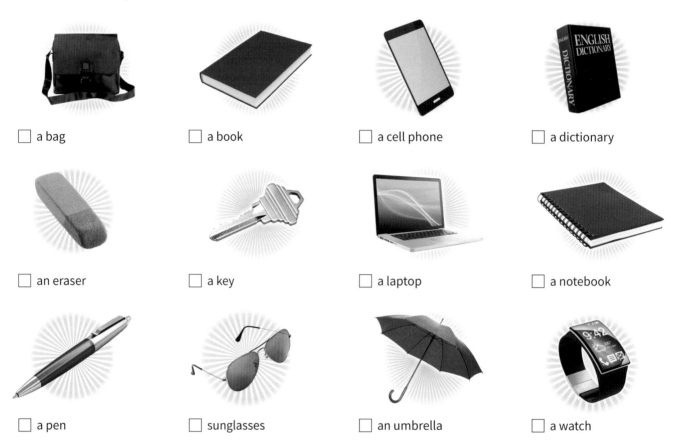

☐ a bag   ☐ a book   ☐ a cell phone   ☐ a dictionary

☐ an eraser   ☐ a key   ☐ a laptop   ☐ a notebook

☐ a pen   ☐ sunglasses   ☐ an umbrella   ☐ a watch

B Check (✓) the things in your classroom. Then compare answers.

2 Language in context What are those?

🎧 Listen to four people talk about everyday items. Circle the items in the conversations.

Pete   Hey, Ling. What's that?

Ling   Oh, it's my watch.

Pete   It's nice. What are those?

Ling   They're my English books.

Susie   Are these your sunglasses?

Pablo   No, they're not.

Susie   Is this your notebook?

Pablo   Yes, it is. Thanks.

3 Grammar 🎧 Demonstratives; articles *a* and *an*; plurals

What's **this**? What's **that**?

It's my dictionary.

Is **this** your dictionary?
Is **that** your dictionary?
Yes, **it is**.   No, **it's not**.

What are **these**? What are **those**?

They're my English books.

Are **these** your English books?
Are **those** your English books?
Yes, **they are**.   No, **they're not**.

Articles *a* and *an*	
a + consonant sound	**a b**ag
an + vowel sound	**an e**raser

Plurals

a book → two book**s**

a watch → two watch**es**

a dictionary → two dictionar**ies**

Note: *Sunglasses* and *glasses* are always plural.

A Complete the conversations with the correct words. Then practice with a partner.

 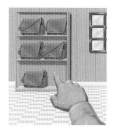  

A What<u>'s this</u>   ?
B   <u>It's a watch.</u>

A What_____ ?
B _____

A What_____ ?
B _____

A What_____ ?
B _____

B **PAIR WORK** Ask and answer questions about everyday items in your classroom.

4 Pronunciation Plurals

🎧 Listen and repeat. Notice that some words have an extra syllable in their plural forms.

Same syllables	Extra syllables
eraser / erasers	actress / actress·es
key / keys	address / address·es
laptop / laptops	watch / watch·es

5 Speaking In my bag

PAIR WORK Ask and answer 10 questions about the everyday items in your bags and in the classroom.

A: Is this your English book?

B: No, it's not. It's my dictionary. What are those?

A: They're my keys.

6 Keep talking!

Go to page 130 for more practice.

I can ask about and identify everyday items. ✓   27

B What's this called in English?

1 Listening Around the classroom

A 🎧 Listen to Bo and Marta ask about new words in English. Number the pictures from 1 to 5.

☐ an alarm clock   ☐ a map   ☐ a marker   ☐ a poster   1 a remote control

B What things in Part A are in your classroom?

2 Interactions Asking about new words

A 🎧 Listen and practice.

Alex	Excuse me. What's this called in English?
Lucy	It's a keychain.
Alex	A keychain? How do you spell that?
Lucy	K-E-Y-C-H-A-I-N.
Alex	Thanks.

B 🎧 Listen to the expressions. Then practice the conversation again with the new expressions.

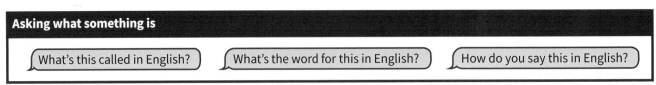

Asking what something is

What's this called in English?   What's the word for this in English?   How do you say this in English?

C **PAIR WORK** Practice the conversation again with the things in Exercise 1.

A: Excuse me. What's this called in English?

B: It's a map.

A: How do you spell that?

3 **Speaking** More everyday items

A 🎧 **Listen and repeat.**

1   a camera
2   a comb
3   a hairbrush
4   a coin

5   a flash drive
6   a wallet
7   a magazine
8   a newspaper

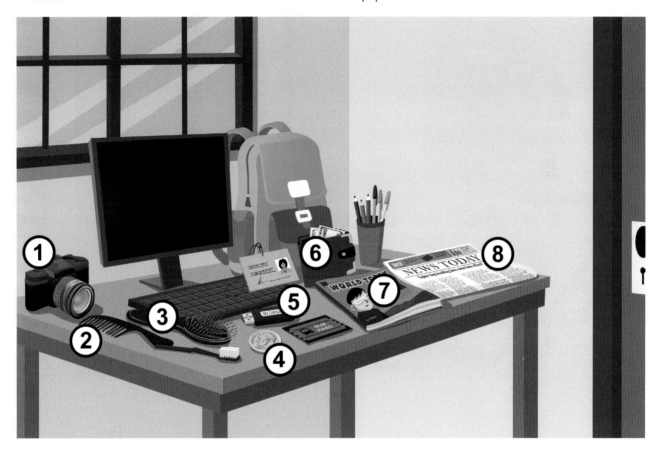

B **PAIR WORK** Cover the words. What is each thing called? Answer with the information you remember.

A: What's this called?

B: I think it's a …

C **PAIR WORK** Ask and answer questions about other things in the picture.

A: What's the word for this in English?

B: It's a student I.D.

A: What's this called?

B: Hmm … I don't know. Let's ask the teacher.

I can ask what something is called in English. ✓

C Clothing

1 Vocabulary Clothes and colors

A 🎧 Listen and repeat.

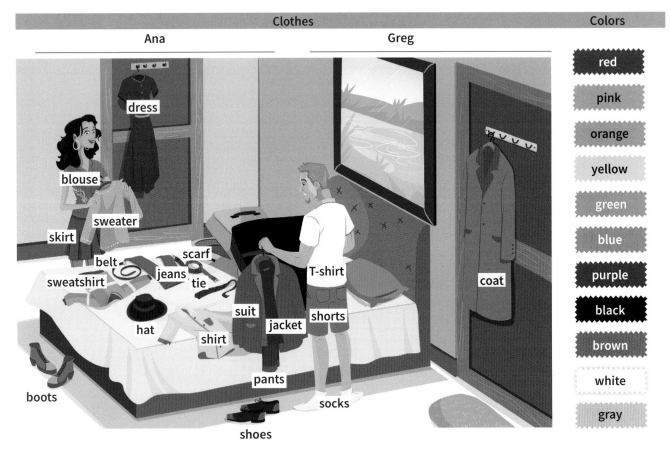

Clothes		Colors
Ana	Greg	

Ana: dress, blouse, sweater, skirt, belt, scarf, jeans, tie, sweatshirt, hat, shirt, boots

Greg: suit, jacket, T-shirt, shorts, pants, socks, shoes, coat

Colors: red, pink, orange, yellow, green, blue, purple, black, brown, white, gray

B **PAIR WORK** Describe a classmate's clothes, but don't say his or her name! Your partner guesses the name. Take turns.

A: His shoes are brown. His T-shirt is red and green. His pants are gray.

B: Is it David?

2 Conversation Whose bag is it?

🎧 Listen and practice.

Greg Excuse me. I think that's my bag.

Laura This bag?

Greg Yes, I think it's mine.

Laura It is? Oh, yes. This bag is black and yellow. Mine is black and green. I'm very sorry.

Greg That's OK. Is that bag yours?

Laura Yes, thank you.

Greg You're welcome.

3 Grammar 🎧 Possessive pronouns; *Whose*; *'s and s'*

It's my bag → It's **mine**.	**Whose** bag is this?
It's your jacket. → It's **yours**.	It's Greg**'s** (bag).
It's his coat. → It's **his**.	**Whose** bag is that?
They're her shoes. → They're **hers**.	It's the student**'s** (bag).
They're our clothes. → They're **ours**.	**Whose** bags are those?
It's their bag. → It's **theirs**.	They're the students**'** (bags).

A Circle the correct words. Then practice with a partner.

1   Whose clothes are these?   They're **your** / **our** / (**ours**).

2   Are these Greg's black shoes?   Yes, they're **his** / **hers** / **theirs**.

3   Is this pink scarf Ana's?   No, it's not **his** / **hers** / **theirs**.

4   Are these bags Greg and Ana's?   Yes, they're **his** / **hers** / **theirs**.

5   Whose red socks are these? Are they yours?   Yes, they're **my** / **mine** / **yours**.

6   Is that my sister's skirt?   No, it's not **mine** / **yours** / **hers**.

B **PAIR WORK** Ask and answer questions about the clothing in Exercise 1.

A: Whose jeans are these?

B: They're Ana's. Whose T-shirt is this?

A: It's …

4 Speaking Yes, it's mine.

CLASS ACTIVITY Put three of your things on a table. Then take three other things and find their owners.

A: Whose hat is this?

B: I think it's Ken's.

A: Is this your hat, Ken?

C: Yes, it's mine.

5 Keep talking!

Student A go to page 131 and Student B go to page 132 for more practice.

I can talk about clothes and possessions. ✓

D Favorite things

1 Reading 🎧

A Look at the things in the pictures. What are they?

B Read Yuna's blog. Circle the things you think Yuna is interested in: sports / art / fashion / movies

YUNA'S BLOG: MY FAVORITE THINGS!

This is my favorite photo of my grandfather. He's from Kyoto.

This T-shirt is my favorite item of clothing. It's from a street market in Mexico.

This is my favorite remote control. It's for my brother. He talks and talks and talks!

Here's a photo of my favorite umbrella. It's my little sister's. She's 8 years old.

This is my favorite painting. It's by Salvador Dalí. He's from Spain.

This backpack is my favorite. It's my friend Marisa's. It's from San Francisco.

C Read the webpage again. Answer the questions.

1 Who is from Kyoto?   *Yuna's grandfather is from Kyoto.*

2 Where is Yuna's T-shirt from?

3 Who talks a lot?

4 How old is Yuna's sister?

5 Who is Yuna's favorite painting by?

6 Where is Marisa's backpack from?

D PAIR WORK Think of three favorite things. Tell your partner.

"My favorite item of clothing is my blue sweatshirt."

32

2 **Listening** It's my favorite.

🎧 Listen to four people talk about their favorite things. Check (✓) the things they describe.

1 a ✓   b ☐

2 a ☐   b ☐

3 a ☐   b ☐

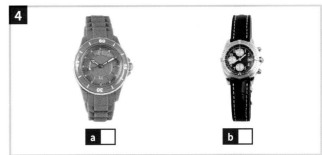

4 a ☐   b ☐

3 **Writing and speaking** My favorite thing

A Draw a picture of your favorite thing. Then answer the questions.

● What is it?
● Where is it from?
● How old is it?
● What color is it?

_____

_____

_____

_____

B Write about your favorite thing. Use the model and your answers in Part A to help you.

My Favorite Thing

My favorite thing is my bag. It's from Cuzco, Peru. I think it's three or four years old. It's purple, white, and yellow. I love it!

C **GROUP WORK** Share your drawings and your writing. Ask and answer questions for more information.

A: Here's a picture of my favorite thing.

B: What is it?

A: It's my bag.

C: Where is it from?

A: It's from Peru.

I can describe my favorite possessions. ✓

Wrap-up

1 Quick pair review

Lesson A Brainstorm!
Make a list of everyday items and the plural forms of the words.
How many do you know? You have two minutes.

Lesson B Test your partner!
Ask your partner what the things are. You have two minutes.

Student A

Student B

Lesson C Do you remember?
Look at your partner's clothes. Then close your eyes and describe them. Take turns.
You have two minutes.

Your shirt is green, and your jeans are blue. I think your socks are white.

Lesson D Find out!
What is one thing both you and your partner have in your bags or desks? Find the thing
and answer the questions. You have two minutes.

- What color is it?
- How old is it?
- Where is it from?

2 In the real world

What's in style? Find a picture of clothes in a magazine. Then write about them.

- What clothes are in the picture?
- What colors are the clothes?

Clothes in "Style Today"
*The woman's sweater in the picture is blue. Her pants
are brown, and her shoes are black. Her bag is . . .*

4 Daily life

Warm Up

A Name the things you see in the picture. Use *That's a / an …* and *Those are … .*

B Say the colors of six things in the picture.

A Getting around

1 Vocabulary Ways of getting around

A 🎧 Listen and repeat.

drive a car

ride a bicycle / bike

ride a motorcycle

take a taxi / cab

take the bus

take the subway

take the train

walk

B 🎧 Listen to five ways of getting around. Number them from 1 to 5.

☐ a bicycle   1 a bus   ☐ a car   ☐ a motorcycle   ☐ a train

2 Language in context Going to work and school

A 🎧 Listen to Mariela describe how she and her family get to work and school.
Underline the ways they get around.

I have a car. I <u>drive</u> to work. I don't take the train.

My husband doesn't drive to work. He has a bike, so he rides his bike.

My kids walk to school. They don't take the bus.

B What about you? Check (✓) the ways you get around.

☐ I drive.   ☐ I take the bus.   ☐ I ride a bike.   ☐ I walk.

3 Grammar 🎧 Simple present statements

Regular verbs	
I **drive** to work.	I **don't take** the train.
You **take** a taxi.	You **don't take** the subway.
He **rides** a bike.	He **doesn't drive** to work.
She **drives**.	She **doesn't walk**.
We **take** the train.	We **don't take** a taxi.
They **walk** to school.	They **don't take** the bus.
Contractions don't = do not	doesn't = does not

Irregular verbs	
I / you / we / they	*he / she*
I **have** a car.	She **has** a car.
You **don't have** a bike.	She **doesn't have** a bike.
We **go** to work.	He **goes** to work.
They **don't go** to school.	He **doesn't go** to school.

A Complete the sentences with the simple present forms of the verbs. Then compare with a partner.

1 I _____take_____ (take) the bus to school. I ___don't walk___ (not / walk).
2 Jonathan _____ (have) a car. He _____ (drive) to work.
3 My parents _____ (take) the train to work. They _____ (go) to the city.
4 My neighbor _____ (ride) a motorcycle to work.
5 Mei-li _____ (not / take) the bus. She _____ (walk).
6 We _____ (not / have) bicycles, and we _____ (not / drive).

B **PAIR WORK** Make five sentences about how your family members and friends get to school or work. Tell your partner.

A: My sister works in a big city. She takes the bus to work.

B: My best friend works in a big city, too. He doesn't take the bus. He drives.

4 Speaking I take the bus.

A Write how you get to school or work in the chart. Add extra information, such as a bus number or a train number.

	Me	Name: _____	Name: _____	Name: _____
To school				
To work				
Extra information				

B **GROUP WORK** Find out how three of your classmates get to school or work. Complete the chart with their information.

A: I take the bus to school. It's the number 16 bus. How about you?

B: I take the bus, too. I take the number 8 bus.

C **GROUP WORK** Tell another group how your classmates get to school or work.

"Daniel takes the number 8 bus to school."

5 Keep talking!

Go to page 133 for more practice.

I can describe how people get around. ✓

37

B What time is it?

1 Telling time

A 🎧 Listen and repeat.

It's twelve o'clock.

It's noon.
It's twelve p.m.

It's midnight.
It's twelve a.m.

It's twelve-oh-five.
It's five after twelve.

It's twelve-fifteen.
It's a quarter after twelve.

It's twelve-thirty.
It's half past twelve.

It's twelve-forty.
It's twenty to one.

It's twelve forty-five.
It's a quarter to one.

B **PAIR WORK** Say the times in two ways.

9:45   7:30   6:03   1:15   11:40.

a.m. = midnight to noon

p.m. = noon to midnight

2 Interactions Time

A 🎧 Listen and practice.

Joe   What time is it?

Mike   It's 9:15. What time is the bus?

Joe   Nine-twenty. We're early.

Keisha   What's the time?

Emily   It's 9:35. What time is our class?

Keisha   It's at 9:30. We're late!

Asking the time

What time is it?   What's the time?

B **PAIR WORK** Practice the conversations again with the times below.

4:15 / 4:45   6:20 / 7:00   10:05 / 10:00   5:45 / 5:30

3 Pronunciation Reduction of *to*

A 🎧 **Listen and repeat. Notice how *to* is pronounced as /tə/.**

/tə/
It's ten to five.

/tə/
It's five to two.

/tə/
It's a quarter to one.

B 🎧 **Listen to the conversations. Then practice them. Reduce *to* to /tə/.**

A Is it five to one?

B No, it's ten to one.

A Is it ten to eight?

B No, it's a quarter to eight.

A Is it a quarter to three?

B No, it's twenty to three.

4 Listening Am I late?

A 🎧 **Listen to five conversations about time. Write the time of each thing.**

1 the movie	2 Rod's class	3 the train	4 the bus	5 Susan's class
10:00				

B 🎧 **Listen again. Are the people early or late? Circle the correct answers.**

1 (early) / late   2 early / late   3 early / late   4 early / late   5 early / late

5 Speaking What time is … ?

A **PAIR WORK** **Interview your partner. Take notes.**

What time is your … ?

favorite class

lunch break

favorite TV show

A: What time is your favorite class?

B: It's at 7:30 a.m. What time is yours?

A: Mine is at 8:00 p.m. It's this class!

B **PAIR WORK** **Tell another classmate about your partner's answers.**

"Ji-sung's favorite class is at 7:30 a.m."

I can ask for and tell the time. ✓

C My routine

1 Vocabulary Days of the week and routines

A 🎧 Listen and repeat.

Weekdays					The weekend	
Monday	Tuesday	Wednesday	Thursday	Friday	Saturday	Sunday

B 🎧 Listen and repeat.

get up

drink coffee

eat breakfast

read the news

go to school

exercise

cook dinner

study

watch TV

go to bed

C **PAIR WORK** What is your routine on weekdays? On weekends? Tell your partner.

"I get up and eat breakfast on weekdays. I go to school. I study . . ."

2 Conversation Monday morning

🎧 Listen and practice.

Tom	It's Monday morning . . . again!
Liz	Do you get up early on weekdays?
Tom	Yes, I do. I get up at 5:30 a.m.
Liz	Wow! That *is* early!
Tom	And I study all morning and afternoon.
Liz	Do you study in the evenings, too?
Tom	No, I don't. I cook dinner, exercise, and go to bed late, after midnight.
Liz	That's not good. What about on weekends?
Tom	On weekends, I sleep!

3 Grammar 🎧 Simple present *yes* / *no* questions

Do you **go** to school on Mondays? 　Yes, I **do**.　　No, I **don't**. **Does** Liz **exercise**? 　Yes, she **does**.　　No, she **doesn't**.	**Do** you and your friends **watch** TV? 　Yes, we **do**.　　No, we **don't**. **Do** your friends **study**? 　Yes, they **do**.　　No, they **don't**.

A Write *yes* / *no* questions with the information below. Then compare with a partner.

　1　(you / get up / 7:00)　　　　　　　　　　　Do you get up at 7:00?

　2　(you / read the news / every day)

　3　(your teacher / drink coffee / in class)

　4　(your parents / watch TV / in the evening)

　5　(your friend / exercise / on weekends)

　6　(you and your friends / study / after midnight)

B **PAIR WORK** Ask and answer the questions in Part A. Answer with your own information.

　A: Do you get up at 7:00?

　B: No, I don't. I get up at 6:00 on weekdays and 9:30 on weekends.

4 Speaking Routines

A **PAIR WORK** Interview your partner. Check (✓) his or her answers.

Do you … ?	Yes	No
cook dinner on weekends	☐	☐
drink coffee after 7:00 p.m.	☐	☐
exercise every day	☐	☐
go to bed late on weekdays	☐	☐
get up early on weekdays	☐	☐
read the news in the evening	☐	☐

　A: Do you cook dinner on weekends?

　B: No, I don't. I cook on weekdays!

B **PAIR WORK** Tell another classmate about your partner's routines.

　A: Does Rita cook dinner on weekends?

　B: No, she doesn't. She cooks on weekdays!

5 Keep talking!

Go to page 134 for more practice.

🎧 **Time expressions**

on Sunday(s)
on Sunday afternoons(s)
on weekdays
on the weekend
on weekends
in the morning(s)
in the afternoon(s)
in the evening(s)
at noon / midnight
at night
before 7:00
after midnight
every day

I can ask and answer questions about routines. ⊘

41

D My weekend

1 Reading 🎧

A Look at the forum question. What's *your* favorite day of the week? Why?

B Read the message board. Whose favorite day is on the weekend?

This week's question:

What's your favorite day of the week?

	busyguy	My favorite day of the week is Saturday. I study from Monday to Friday. On Saturday, I get up late.
	trish06	Not Saturday or Sunday. I work from noon to 4:00 on those days. In the evening, I study. My favorite day is Wednesday, because I don't work on Wednesdays.
	JasonFan	Monday. I watch my favorite TV show every Monday. It has my favorite actor. The show is called "Life with Jason." It's on at 8:00.
	Ricardo	Monday?! No way! Saturday, Saturday, Saturday! We don't go to school on Saturdays.
	SuperDad45	Sunday! I get up late, read the news, and have coffee. Then my son and daughter cook breakfast for my wife and me.
	michiko3	I have two favorite days – Tuesday and Thursday. I have an art class after work on those days, and my teacher is very nice.

C Read the forum again. What's each person's favorite day? Why? Complete the chart.

	Favorite day(s)	Why?
busyguy	Saturday	gets up late
trish06		
JasonFan		
Ricardo		
SuperDad45		
michiko3		

D **CLASS ACTIVITY** What's your class's favorite day? Vote and discuss your answer.

2 **Listening** Angela's routine

A 🎧 Listen to Angela talk about her routine on weekends. Circle the activities she does.

Saturdays		Sundays	
(work)	watch TV	get up late	exercise
go to class	go to bed late	study	cook

B 🎧 Listen again. Write one more thing Angela does on Saturdays and on Sundays.

On Saturdays: _____   On Sundays: _____

3 **Writing** About my weekend

A Complete the chart with information about your weekend routine. Include two activities you do and two activities you don't do.

Saturdays

Activities I do:
• _____
• _____

Activities I don't do:
• _____
• _____

Sundays

Activities I do:
• _____
• _____

Activities I don't do:
• _____
• _____

My Weekend Routine

On Saturdays, I get up late and watch TV. I don't study and I don't go to work. On Sundays, …

B Write about your weekend routine. Use the model and your answers in Part A to help you.

C GROUP WORK Share your writing. Ask and answer questions for more information.

4 **Speaking** Are you busy?

A Add two questions about routines to the survey. Then circle your answers.

Are you busy?	Me		You	
1 Do you study English every weekend?	Yes	No	Yes	No
2 Do you go to work on the weekend?	Yes	No	Yes	No
3 Do you get up before 7:00 on the weekend?	Yes	No	Yes	No
4 Do you exercise on the weekend?	Yes	No	Yes	No
5	Yes	No	Yes	No
6	Yes	No	Yes	No

B PAIR WORK Interview your partner. Circle his or her answers. Is your partner busy?

I can describe the things I do on weekends.

43

Wrap-up

1 Quick pair review

Lesson A `Brainstorm!`
Make a list of ways of getting around. How many do you know? You have one minute.

Lesson B `Test your partner!`
Say four different times. Can your partner write them correctly? Check his or her answers. You have two minutes.

Lesson C `Guess!`
Say a time and a day. Can your partner guess your routine at that time? Take turns.
You have two minutes.

A: Two o'clock on Monday.

B: Do you exercise at 2:00 on Monday?

A: No.

B: Do you study?

A: Yes.

Lesson D `Find out!`
What are three things both you and your partner do on weekends?
You have two minutes.

A: I exercise on Saturday mornings. How about you?

B: No, I don't. I go to bed late on Saturdays. How about you?

A: Yes, I do!

2 In the real world

What time is it around the world? Go online and find the local time in these cities.

Beijing	Cairo	Los Angeles	Rio de Janeiro	Tokyo
Buenos Aires	London	Mexico City	Sydney	Toronto

What time is it now?
It is nine o'clock in the evening in Beijing now.
In Buenos Aires, it's …

Beijing

5 Free time

Warm Up

A Look at the pictures. Make two sentences about each one.

B When do you have free time? Write the times.

	Monday	Tuesday	Wednesday	Thursday	Friday	Saturday	Sunday
a.m.							
p.m.							

A Online habits

1 Vocabulary Online activities

A 🎧 Listen and repeat.

☐ use social media

☐ check email

☐ download apps

☐ play games

☐ stream music

☐ watch videos

☐ shop online

☐ post photos

B **PAIR WORK** Check (✓) the things you do online. Then tell your partner.

"I use social media, check email, and play games. How about you?"

2 Language in context Habits survey

A 🎧 Read the survey about online habits. Circle the online activities.

Habits Survey

1 Do you ever shop online?
   ☑ Yes, I often shop online.
   ☐ Yes, I sometimes shop online.
   ☐ No, I never shop online.

2 Do you ever post photos?
   ☐ Yes, I often post photos.
   ☑ Yes, I sometimes post photos.
   ☐ No, I never post photos.

3 Do you ever play games?
   ☐ Yes, I often play games.
   ☐ Yes, I sometimes play games.
   ☑ No, I never play games.

B What about you? Do you do the online activities in the survey?

3 Grammar 🎧 Adverbs of frequency

always	100%	Do you **ever** shop online?
usually		Yes, I sometimes shop online.
often		Yes, I sometimes do.
I	shop online.	No, I never shop online.
sometimes		No, I never do.
hardly ever		
never	0%	

A Rewrite the conversations with the adverbs of frequency. Then practice with a partner.

1 A Do you watch movies online? (ever)   *Do you ever watch movies online?*

B Yes, I watch movies online. (often)

2 A Do you check email in class? (ever)

B No, I check email in class. (never)

3 A Do you play games online? (ever)

B Yes, I do. (usually)

4 A Do you download apps? (ever)

B No, I do that. (hardly ever)

B PAIR WORK Ask and answer the questions in Part A. Answer with your own information.

A: *Do you ever watch movies online?*

B: *Yes, I sometimes do.*

4 Speaking Often, sometimes, or never?

A 🎧 Complete the chart with information about your online habits. Use the ideas in Exercise 1 and your own ideas.

I often …	I sometimes …	I never …

B GROUP WORK Compare your online habits.

A: *I often play games online.*

B: *Oh? I never do that.*

C: *I sometimes do.*

5 Keep talking!

Go to page 135 for more practice.

I can talk about my online habits. ✓   47

B How much is it?

1 Prices

A 🎧 Listen and repeat.

$79.00   =   seventy-nine dollars

$79.95   =   seventy-nine dollars and ninety-five cents

         OR   seventy-nine ninety-five

$379.95   =   three hundred seventy-nine dollars and ninety-five cents

         OR   three seventy-nine ninety-five

B 🎧 Listen and practice.

A: How much is this?

B: It's $54.89.

A: How much are these?

B: They're $234.99.

A: How much is that watch?

B: It's only $109.25.

C **PAIR WORK** Practice the conversations again. Say the prices in a different way.

2 Interactions   At the store

A 🎧 Listen and practice.

Salesperson	Hello.
Margaret	Hi.
Salesperson	Can I help you?
Margaret	No, thanks. I'm just looking.

Salesperson	Can I help you?
Renato	Yes, please. How much is this camera?
Salesperson	It's $169.50.
Renato	Thanks.

B 🎧 Listen to the expressions. Then practice the conversations again with the new expressions.

Declining help

No, thanks. I'm just looking.

No. I'm fine, thanks.

Accepting help

Yes, please.

Yes, thanks.

3 **Pronunciation** Thirteen or thirty?

A 🎧 Listen and repeat. Notice the difference in stress in the numbers.

B 🎧 Listen to four conversations about prices. Circle the correct prices.

1 ($14)/ $40   3 $17 / $70

2 $16 / $60   4 $19 / $90

C **PAIR WORK** Say a number from the chart. Your partner points to it. Take turns.

Last syllable	First syllable
13 thir**teen**	30 **thir**ty
14 four**teen**	40 **for**ty
15 fif**teen**	50 **fif**ty
16 six**teen**	60 **six**ty
17 seven**teen**	70 **se**venty
18 eigh**teen**	80 **eigh**ty
19 nine**teen**	90 **nine**ty

4 **Listening** Can I help you?

A 🎧 Listen to four conversations in a store. Check (✓) the words you hear.

1 ☑ camera   2 ☐ shirts   3 ☐ bag   4 ☐ scarf

☐ cell phone   ☐ skirt   ☐ bags   ☐ shorts

☐ laptop   ☐ T-shirt   ☐ belt   ☐ skirt

B 🎧 Listen to a salesperson offer help to four customers. Do the customers accept or decline help? Circle the correct answers.

1 (accept)/ decline   2 accept / decline   3 accept / decline   4 accept / decline

5 **Speaking** Role play

CLASS ACTIVITY Role-play the situation. Then change roles.

Group A: You are salespeople. Offer help to the customers. Answer questions about prices.

Group B: You are customers. Decline help three times. Then accept help three times and ask for the prices of three items.

$168.95

$23.99

$877.50

$400.89

$119.00

$9.25

A: Can I help you?

B: No, thanks. I'm just looking.

OR

A: Can I help you?

B: Yes, please. How much . . . ?

I can accept and decline help. ✓

C What do you do for fun?

1 Vocabulary Leisure activities and places

A 🎧 Listen and repeat.

eat out

go dancing

go shopping

hang out

play soccer

watch movies

B 🎧 Listen and repeat.

at a club

at a restaurant

at home

at the mall

at the park

C PAIR WORK Do you do the activities in Part A? Where? Tell your partner.

A: I watch movies at home. Do you?

B: Yes, I do. I watch movies at the mall, too.

2 Conversation In our free time

🎧 Listen and practice.

Annie What do you do for fun, Chad?

Chad Oh, I hang out with friends.

Annie Yeah? Where do you hang out?

Chad At the mall. We sometimes watch a movie or go shopping. What about you?

Annie I play soccer in the park.

Chad Sounds fun. Who do you play with?

Annie My brother and his friends. Actually, we need another player. Are you interested?

Chad Yeah!

3 Grammar 🎧 Simple present *Wh-* questions with *do*

What do you do for fun?
     I hang out.
Where do you hang out?
     At the mall.
How do you get there?
     We take the bus.
	Who do you play soccer with?
	     My brother and his friends.
	When do you usually play soccer?
	     We usually play on weekends.
	Why do you play soccer?
	     Because it's my favorite sport.

A Read the answers. Write *Wh-* questions. Then practice with a partner.

1 How do you get to class? _____ I take the bus to class.

2 _____ I eat out on Friday night.

3 _____ I play sports with my brother.

4 _____ I go shopping at the mall.

5 _____ My friends and I watch movies on Saturday.

6 _____ I sometimes study with my friends.

B PAIR WORK Ask and answer the questions in Part A. Answer with your own information.

A: How do you get to class?

B: I usually walk, but I sometimes take the subway.

4 Speaking Tell me more!

A PAIR WORK Interview your partner. Take notes.

Questions	Name: _____
1 When do you usually check your email?	
2 What time do you go to bed on Sundays?	
3 When do you chat with friends?	
4 Who do you eat out with? Where do you go?	
5 Where do you go shopping? How do you get there?	
6 What do you do for fun on weekends? Why?	

B PAIR WORK Tell another classmate about your partner's answers. Are any of your partners' answers the same?

A: Celia usually checks her email at night.

B: Luis checks his email at night, too.

5 Keep talking!

Go to page 136 for more practice.

D Online fun

1 Reading 🎧

A Look at the pictures in the article. What do you see?

B Read the article. What's the best title? Check (✓) the correct answer.

☐ New Websites   ☐ Chat   ☐ Fun Online Activities

Try one of these activities in your free time.

Buy and Sell

What do you want? A new video game? A new phone? What *don't* you want? Your old jeans? Your old schoolbooks? Buy and sell things online!

Where is your best friend from elementary school now? Does your friend live in your city? Search his or her name, and find your friend.

Do you have pictures or movies on your cell phone or camera? Post them! Upload your favorite photos and videos for friends.

Tour a museum from your home! Go to the Egyptian Museum in Cairo, Barcelona's Picasso Museum, or Kyoto's National Museum.

Where do you want to go? Search the address and city, and find a map. Get directions to stores, parks, or a new restaurant.

Do you want to discover a new band or listen to your favorite singer on your cellphone? Use an app to stream music.

C Read the article again. Where do the headings go? Write them in the article.

Map it!   Take a Tour   Share Photos and Videos

Get Music   ✓ Buy and Sell   Find an Old Friend

D **PAIR WORK** What activities do you do online? Tell your partner.

"I hardly ever sell things online, but I sometimes buy clothes online."

2 Listening Four websites

A 🎧 Listen to Helena and Michael talk about the pictures on four websites. Number the pictures from 1 to 4.

B 🎧 Listen again. Correct the false sentences.

                 photos
1 Michael looks at ~~videos~~ of Stephen Curry.

2 The Museum of Modern Art is in Paris.

3 Michael shops on the website.

4 Helena often uploads videos.

3 Writing Let's chat!

A Choose a topic for a chat: free time, online activities, or school. Write a question about your topic.

B GROUP WORK Send your question to the classmate on the right in a text message or on paper. Read and answer your classmate's question. Continue to read and answer all of the questions in your group.

Sandra:	What do you do in your free time?
Jaemin:	I watch TV and play video games. My favorite video game is "Soccer Star."
Roberto:	I hardly ever play video games. I usually watch TV at night. My favorite show is …

C CLASS ACTIVITY Tell the class about your chat.

4 Speaking My favorite website

A GROUP WORK Add a question about online habits to the list. Then ask and answer the questions.

- What's your favorite website or app?
- What other websites or apps do you usually use?
-
- What news websites do you read?
- What blogs do you read?

B CLASS ACTIVITY Share your information. Which websites and apps are popular?

I can discuss how I use technology. ✓

Wrap-up

1 Quick pair review

Lesson A `Brainstorm!`

Make a list of online activities. How many do you know? You have one minute.

Lesson B `Test your partner!`

Write three prices and say them to your partner. Can your partner write them correctly?
Check his or her answers. You have two minutes.

My prices	My partner's prices
_____ _____	_____ _____
_____ _____	_____ _____

Lesson C `Find out!`

What are three activities both you and your partner do for fun? You have two minutes.

A: I play soccer for fun. Do you?

B: No, I don't play soccer. Do you go shopping for fun?

A: Yes, sometimes.

Lesson D `Do you remember?`

Complete the sentences with the correct words. You have one minute.

✓ Buy	Find	Share	Take

1 _____Buy_____ and sell online.   3 _____ an old friend.

2 _____ photos and videos.   4 _____ a tour.

2 In the real world

How much are they? Find two different prices for each of these items.
Then write about them.

a belt	jeans	a small camera
a downloaded song	a laptop	an umbrella

Different Prices

A black belt is $29.99 at Style Shop.
It's $20.00 at Kelly's Accessories.
A downloaded song is ...

6 Work and play

Warm Up

A Where do the people usually work?

B Do you know any of the jobs in the pictures? Do you know any other jobs?

A What does she do?

1 Vocabulary Jobs

A 🎧 Match the jobs and the people. Then listen and check your answers.

a	accountant	c	doctor	e	flight attendant	g	nurse	i	police officer	k	waitress
b	cook / chef	d	electrician	✓f	waiter	h	pilot	j	receptionist	l	taxi driver

B **PAIR WORK** Point to people in the pictures and ask what their jobs are. Your partner says the jobs. Take turns.

A: What's his job?

B: He's a waiter.

2 Language in context At work

A 🎧 Read two job profiles. What are their jobs?

Lucia Ortega works in a hospital from 11:00 p.m. to 7:00 a.m. What does Lucia do? She's a nurse.

Henry Jenkins works in an office. He's an accountant. What company does Henry work for? He works for A1 Accountants.

B What about you? Do you have a job? What is it? What jobs do you think are interesting?

3 Grammar 🎧 Simple present *Wh-* questions with *does*

What does Lucia **do**?
   She's a nurse.
 When does she **work**?
   She works from 11:00 to 7:00.
	Where does Henry **work**?
	   He works in an office.
	 What company **does** Henry **work** for?
	   He works for A1 Accountants.

A Complete the conversations with the correct words. Then practice with a partner.

1. A   ___What___ does your brother ___do___?
   B   Oh, Tom's a doctor.
   A   Really? _____ does he _____?
   B   He works in a hospital.

2. A   _____ does Sue _____?
   B   On Mondays, Wednesdays, and Fridays.
   A   And _____ company does she _____ for?
   B   She works for Town Bank.

B **PAIR WORK** Write questions about Mr. Miller, Lisa, and Nicole. Then ask and answer them.

Mr. Miller

Lisa

Nicole

What *does Mr. Miller do*?   What _____?   Where _____?

Where _____?   When _____?   What company _____?

    A: What *does Mr. Miller do?*

    B: He's an English teacher.

4 Speaking People's jobs

CLASS ACTIVITY Add two jobs to the chart. Then find classmates who know people with those jobs. **Ask for more information.**

Job	Classmate	Person	Extra information
chef			
nurse			
police officer			
taxi driver			

    A: Do you know a chef?   **A:** Where does he work?

    B: Yes. My friend Marco is a chef.   **B:** He works at Speedy Sushi.

5 Keep talking!

Go to page 137 for more practice.

B Can I speak to … ?

Interactions On the phone

A Look at the pictures. Where does Michael work?

B 🎧 Listen and practice.

Michael	Good morning, Quality Hotel.
Ashley	Hello. Can I speak to Laura Diaz?
Michael	Who is this, please?
Ashley	It's Ashley Tillman.

Michael	Just a minute, please. . . . Oh, I'm sorry, Ms. Diaz is busy at the moment.
Ashley	All right. Thank you.

C 🎧 Listen to the expressions. Then practice the conversation again with the new expressions.

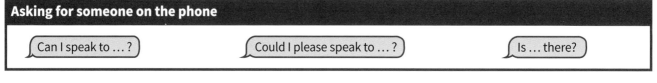

Asking for someone on the phone

Can I speak to … ?   Could I please speak to … ?   Is … there?

Having someone wait

Just a minute, please.   Hold on, please.   One moment, please.

D PAIR WORK Practice the conversation again with the names below.

Gabriela Garcia

Anthony Davis

Kumiko Takahashi

Roberto Santos

A: *Good morning, Quality Hotel.*

B: *Hello. Can I speak to Gabriela Garcia?*

A: *Who is this, please?*

2 **Listening** A busy woman

A 🎧 Listen to Kevin call Star Computers on five different days. Where is Ellen Astor each day?
Number the pictures from 1 to 5.

at lunch

in a meeting

on another line

on vacation

with a customer

B 🎧 Listen again. How does Kevin ask to speak to Ellen Astor? Number the questions
from 1 to 5.

_____ Is Ms. Astor there?

_____ Could I please speak to . . . ?

___1___ Can I please speak to Ellen Astor?

_____ Can I speak to Ellen Astor?

_____ Could I speak to Ms. Astor, please?

3 **Speaking** Role play

PAIR WORK Role-play the situation. Then change roles.

Student A: You are a receptionist at Sun Travel. Answer the phone. Tell the caller to wait,
and then say why the person can't talk.

Student B: Call Sun Travel. Imagine someone you know works there. Ask to speak to the person.

A: Hello, Sun Travel.

B: Hi. Can I please speak to Jackie Miller?

A: Of course. Just a minute, please …
I'm sorry. Jackie's with a customer.

B: Oh, OK. Thanks.

I **can** ask for someone on the telephone. ✓

I **can** have someone wait. ✓

C Can you sing?

1 Vocabulary Abilities

A 🎧 Listen and repeat.

dance

draw

fix computers

paint

play the guitar

sing

speak French

swim

B **PAIR WORK** What things do you sometimes do? Tell your partner.

2 Conversation Top talent?

🎧 Listen and practice.

Host	Welcome to *Top Talent*. What's your name, please?
Pamela	Hello. My name is Pamela Wells.
Host	Tell us, can you sing, Pamela?
Pamela	No, I can't sing at all.
Host	Well, can you play an instrument? The guitar? The piano?
Pamela	No, I can't.
Host	You can't sing and you can't play an instrument. What *can* you do, Pamela?
Pamela	I can dance!
Host	Great! Let's see.

3 Grammar 🎧 *Can* for ability; *and, but,* and *or*

I		
You		
He	**can**	dance very well.
She	**can't**	sing at all.
We		
They		

Can you sing?

Yes, I **can**.   No, I **can't**.

What **can** Pamela do?

She **can** dance, **and** she **can** swim.

She **can** dance, **but** she **can't** swim.

She **can't** sing **or** play an instrument.

A Read the answers. Write the questions. Then practice with a partner.

1 Can Jenny swim? _____   No, Jenny can't swim.

2 _____   Billy can fix computers.

3 _____   Yes, Tom and Jill can sing very well.

4 _____   No, I can't play an instrument.

5 _____   Jay and I can dance and speak French.

6 _____   No, Sally can't paint at all.

B PAIR WORK Make six sentences about Frank with *and, but,* or *or*. Tell your partner.

Frank's Abilities

☑ draw   ☒ sing   ☑ swim

☒ paint   ☒ dance   ☑ play the guitar

"Frank can draw, but …"

4 Pronunciation *Can* and *can't*

A 🎧 Listen and repeat. Notice the pronunciation of *can* /kən/ and *can't* /kænt/.

I can draw.   I can't paint.   I can draw, but I can't paint.

B 🎧 Listen to the conversations. Do you hear *can* or *can't*? Circle the correct answers.

1 can / (can't)   2 can / can't   3 can / can't   4 can / can't

5 Speaking *Can you paint?*

A PAIR WORK Add two abilities to the chart. Then interview your partner. Check (✓) the things he or she can do.

Can you … ?			
paint	cook	sing in English	ride a bicycle
draw	dance	play an instrument	
swim	drive	fix a car	

B PAIR WORK Tell another classmate about your partner's abilities. Can your partner do something that you can't? What is it?

6 Keep talking!

Go to page 138 for more practice.

I can describe my talents and abilities. ✓

D Work and study

1 Reading 🎧

A Look at the pictures. Where are these people? Guess.

B Read the article. Which jobs include travel?

FUN JOBS

WATER SLIDE TESTER

Every new water slide needs a water slide tester! Your job: visit new water parks and be the first person down the water slide. It's fun, and you can swim every day on the job.

PANDA NANNY

A panda nanny works with baby pandas in China. Usually, you hang out and play games with pandas. You often cook dinner for them, too. Sometimes you even wear a panda suit!

CRUISE SHIP WAITER

A cruise ship waiter works in a restaurant on a ship. Your working day is long – you often work breakfast, lunch, and dinner – but you can travel to many countries and meet lots of people.

VIDEO GAME DESIGNER

A video game designer works for a software company and helps to make new video games. Usually, you are in a large team, and you work on one game for many months. Video game companies need artists, writers, and computer programmers.

C Read the article again. Answer the questions.

1 Which job has long hours? *cruise ship waiter*
2 In which job do you work on a computer?
3 Which job is only in China?
4 In which job do you travel to many countries?
5 In which job can you swim every day?
6 In which job do you play with animals?

D **PAIR WORK** Which job is your favorite? Which job sounds hard? Can you think of other fun jobs? Tell your partner.

2 Listening Exciting opportunities

A 🎧 Listen to two students discuss three advertisements. Number them from 1 to 3.

Volunteer!

Are you interested in animals? Can you swim? _____ with turtles in Costa Rica. Work _____ to Saturday, 6:00 a.m. to _____ p.m. For more information, send an email to **CRVolunteer@cup.edu**

□

Be an Intern

Are you 18 to _____ years old? Can you speak Chinese, _____, Japanese, or English? Be an intern at a theme _____ in Hong Kong! Email us at **hongkong@cup.com/intern**

□

Study and Work

Can you cook? Come to Rome. Study Italian in the morning and work in a restaurant in the _evening_. See the city in your _____ time! _____ salary. Contact us at **study&work@cambridge.org**

1

B 🎧 Listen again. Complete the sentences with the correct words.

3 Writing My abilities

A Make lists of things you can and can't do well. Then write a paragraph about your abilities. Use the model and your lists to help you.

> ### My Abilities
>
> I can play sports. I can play basketball and tennis very well. My favorite sport is soccer, but I can't play it very well. I can't play golf at all!

B **PAIR WORK** Share your paragraphs. Ask and answer questions for more information.

4 Speaking How well can you … ?

GROUP WORK Discuss the opportunities in Exercise 1, Exercise 2, or your own ideas.

- What abilities do you need in each program?
- How well can you do each thing? (very well? well? not well? not at all?)
- Are any of the programs right for you?

I can talk about study and work programs. ✓

Wrap-up

1 Quick pair review

Lesson A Guess!

Describe a job, but don't say what it is. Can your partner guess it? Take turns.
You have two minutes.

A: This person drives a car.

B: Is he a police officer?

A: No. The car is yellow in New York City.

B: Is he a taxi driver?

A: Yes.

Lesson B Brainstorm!

Make a list of ways to ask for someone on the phone and have someone wait.
You have two minutes.

Lesson C Find out!

What are two things both you and your partner can do? What are two things you can't do?
You have two minutes.

A: Can you cook?

B: Not really. Can you?

A: No, I can't!

Lesson D Do you remember?

Are the sentences true or false? Write *T* (true) or *F* (false). You have two minutes.

1   A water slide tester hangs out and plays games. ___F___

2   A panda nanny travels to many countries. _____

3   A cruise ship waiter meets lots of people. _____

4   A video game designer works on a ship. _____

2 In the real world

Go online and find information in English about a program in a different country. Then write about it.

● What is the name of the program?

● Where is the program?

● What kind of program is it?

● What do people do in the program?

The Peace Corps

The Peace Corps is an international program.
Americans volunteer in many countries.
They help build things and teach people.

7 Food

Warm Up

A Match the words and the pictures.

1 Italian food ___C___   2 Mexican food _____   3 Chinese food _____   4 Japanese food _____

B Name ten food words you know.

A Breakfast, lunch, and dinner

1 Vocabulary Food

A 🎧 Match the words and the pictures. Then listen and check your answers.

a	apples	e	carrots	i	eggs	m	pasta
b	bananas	f	cereal	j	fish	n	potatoes
c	beans	✓ g	cheese	k	milk	o	rice
d	beef	h	chicken	l	noodles	p	tomatoes

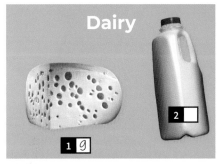
Dairy
1 g 2 □

Vegetables
3 □ 4 □ 5 □

Fruit
6 □ 7 □

Grains
8 □ 9 □ 10 □ 11 □

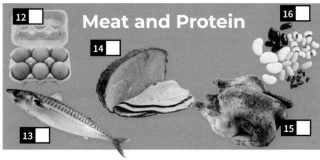
Meat and Protein
12 □ 13 □ 14 □ 15 □ 16 □

B **PAIR WORK** Do you ever eat the food in Part A? Tell your partner.

"I often eat apples. I sometimes eat eggs. I never eat noodles."

2 Language in context Favorite meals

A 🎧 Listen to three people talk about their favorite meals. Underline the food.

I love breakfast. I usually eat some cereal, but I don't have any milk with it. I also eat an apple.

My favorite meal is lunch. I don't have a lot of time, so I often just get some noodles.

My favorite meal of the day is dinner. A typical dinner for me is rice and beans with some beef.

B What about you? What's your favorite meal of the day? What do you eat?

3 Grammar 🎧 Count and noncount nouns; *some* and *any*

Count nouns	Noncount nouns
an apple apples a tomato tomatoes	milk rice
Do you have **any** apples?	Do you have **any** milk?
Yes, I have **some** (apples).	Yes, I have **some** (milk).
No, I don't have **any** (apples).	No, I don't have **any** (milk).

A Complete the chart with the food words from Exercise 1. Then compare with a partner.

Count nouns		Noncount nouns	
apples		milk	
tomatoes		cereal	

B Circle the correct words. Then practice with a partner.

A What do you want for lunch, Amy?

B Let's just make **some** / **any** pasta.

A Good idea. We have **some** / **any** pasta.

B Let's see. We have **some** / **any** carrots.
We don't have **some** / **any** tomatoes.

A OK, I can get **some** / **any** at the store. What else?

B Do we have **some** / **any** cheese?

A No, we don't have **some** / **any**. I can get **some** / **any**.

C **PAIR WORK** Practice the conversation again.
Use other food words from Exercise 1.

4 Speaking What do you eat?

A Write your answers to the questions in the chart.

What do you often eat for … ?	Me	Name: _____	Name: _____
breakfast			
lunch			
dinner			

B **GROUP WORK** Interview two classmates. Complete the chart with their answers.

5 Keep talking!

Go to page 139 for more practice.

I can say what meals I eat. ✓

B I like Chinese food!

1 Interactions Likes and dislikes

A Look at the pictures. Where are Maria and Tom?

B 🎧 Listen and practice.

Maria   Look! They have Italian food here.

Tom   Do you like Italian food?

Maria   I don't like pizza at all, but I love pasta.

Tom   I don't like Italian food.

Maria   How about Chinese food?

Tom   Good idea. I like Chinese food!

Maria   I really like the noodles here.

Tom   Great! We can eat lunch at this restaurant.

C 🎧 Listen to the expressions. Then practice the conversation again with the new expressions.

Expressing dislikes

I don't like …   I don't like … at all.   I hate … !

Expressing likes

I like …   I really like …   I love … !

D **PAIR WORK** Look at Maria's and Tom's likes and dislikes. Are they the same as yours? Tell your partner.

Maria	fish	Mexican food	Japanese food	milk	beans	beef
Tom	cheese	carrots	Chinese food	Italian food	French food	eggs

"Maria loves fish, but I don't like fish at all."

2 Pronunciation Word stress

A 🎧 Listen and repeat. Notice the stress in the words.

●	●•	•●•
cheese	**a**pple	ba**na**na
beans	**chi**cken	po**ta**to
beef	**noo**dles	to**ma**to

B 🎧 Listen. Complete the chart with the correct words.

dairy   fruit   Italian   meat   pasta

3 Listening I love it!

A 🎧 Listen to four conversations about food. Check (✓) the words you hear.

1 ☐ beans　2 ☐ cheese　3 ☐ noodles　4 ☐ bananas
　 ✓ beef　　　☐ chicken　　☐ potatoes　　☐ carrots
　 ✓ pasta　　 ☐ eggs　　　☐ tomatoes　　☐ cereal

B 🎧 Listen again. Do the two speakers like the same things? Circle the correct answers.

1 yes / (no)　　　2 yes / no　　　3 yes / no　　　4 yes / no

4 Speaking What do you like?

A Make a list of food you like and food you don't like.

Food I like
☺
😄
😍

Food I don't like
☹
😖
😵

B **PAIR WORK** Tell your partner about the food you like and don't like. Ask and answer questions for more information.

A: I really like fish.

B: Do you cook fish at home?

A: No, I don't. I eat fish in restaurants.

I can say what I like and dislike. ✓

C Meals

1 Vocabulary More food

A 🎧 Label the pictures with the correct words. Then listen and check your answers.

dumplings	✓ hot dogs	pizza	soup	sushi
hamburgers	pancakes	salad	spaghetti	tacos

1   hot dogs

2 _____

3 _____

4 _____

5 _____

6 _____

7 _____

8 _____

9 _____

10 _____

B **PAIR WORK** Which food in Part A do you like? Which food don't you like? Compare your answers.

A: I really like dumplings. Do you?

B: Yes, I like dumplings, too. Do you like ... ?

2 Conversation I eat pizza every day.

🎧 Listen and practice.

Megan What is that?

David Pizza. My father is a pizza chef.

Megan Really? So how often do you eat pizza?

David I eat pizza every day. It's my favorite food!

Megan I don't eat pizza very often, but it looks interesting. What's on it?

David Cheese, tomatoes, black beans, and fish.

Megan Yuck!

David Have some. It's really good.

Megan No, thanks. I'm not very hungry.

3 Grammar 🎧 *How often;* time expressions

How often do you eat pizza?		
I eat pizza	every day. once a week. twice a month. three times a month. once in a while.	I don't eat pizza **very often**. I **never** eat pizza.

A Look at Matt's menu. Answer the questions. Then practice with a partner.

WEEKLY MENU PLANNER 🍴
Matt's menu

	Monday	Tuesday	Wednesday	Thursday	Friday	Saturday	Sunday
Breakfast	cereal	eggs	cereal	eggs	cereal	pancakes	pancakes
Lunch	soup	pizza	soup	sushi	soup	tacos	sushi
Dinner	dumplings	chicken	beef	chicken	pizza	spaghetti	hamburgers

1 How often does Matt eat hamburgers for dinner?   He eats hamburgers once a week.

2 How often does Matt eat soup for lunch?

3 How often does Matt eat pancakes?

4 How often does Matt eat hot dogs?

5 How often does Matt eat sushi for lunch?

6 How often does Matt eat dumplings for dinner?

B **PAIR WORK** Make six sentences about your eating habits with different time expressions. Tell your partner.

"I eat spaghetti once a month."

4 Speaking Eating habits

A Add three food words to the chart. Then answer the questions.

B **PAIR WORK** Interview your partner. Complete the chart with his or her answers.

C **PAIR WORK** Compare your information with another partner.

"Kazu eats hot dogs once a week, but I eat them once in a while."

How often do you eat ...?	Me	Name: _____
hot dogs		
salad		
tacos		

5 Keep talking!

Go to page 140 for more practice.

I can talk about my eating habits. ✓

D Favorite food

1 Reading 🎧

A Look at the pictures in the magazine article. Can you name the food?

B Read the article. What's the best title? Check (✓) the correct answer.

☐ Meal Times   ☐ My Favorite Food   ☐ Dinner Around the World

LETTERS FROM OUR READERS

Heather
United States

I love nachos. I make them once a week. I just buy some tortilla chips and put cheese, beef, tomatoes, and onions on top. Then I cook it in the microwave.

♡ ◯   34 likes   Follow

Jae-sun
South Korea

I like dumplings a lot. You can buy good dumplings in restaurants, but I usually eat my mother's dumplings. They're delicious! I eat them for lunch four or five times a month.

♡ ◯   23 likes   Follow

Carlos
Argentina

My wife and I go to our favorite ice cream shop three times a month. They have many flavors, but we always get chocolate ice cream. It's our favorite.

♡ ◯   55 likes   Follow

Olga
Sweden

I really like pancakes, but we don't eat them for breakfast. We eat them after dinner. We usually eat them two or three times a month. I like to eat them with jam.

♡ ◯   68 likes   Follow

C Read the article again. Complete the chart with the correct information.

Name	Favorite food	How often they have it
Heather	nachos	once a week
Jae-sun		
Carlos		
Olga		

D **PAIR WORK** Imagine you can have one food in Part A right now. Which food do you want? Why? Tell your partner.

"I want dumplings. I love South Korean food. Vegetable dumplings are my favorite."

2 Listening A meal in Sweden

A 🎧 Listen to Olga describe a typical meal in Sweden. Which meal does she talk about? Check (✓) the correct answer.

☐ breakfast   ☐ lunch   ☐ dinner

B 🎧 Listen again. Circle the words you hear.

beans	(bread)	cheese	fish	milk	pancakes
beef	cereal	eggs	fruit	noodles	potatoes

3 Writing A typical meal

A Think of a typical meal in your country. Answer the questions.

1 What do people drink? _____

2 What do people eat? _____

3 Do *you* usually eat it? _____

4 Why or why not? _____

B Write about a typical meal in your country. Use the model and your answers in Part A to help you.

C **CLASS ACTIVITY** Post your writing around the room. Read your classmates' writing. Who describes similar meals?

A Japanese Breakfast

People in Japan usually drink green tea for breakfast. They eat fish, rice, soup, salad, and pickles. It's a healthy and delicious breakfast, but I don't eat this. I usually drink orange juice and eat cereal and fruit for breakfast.

4 Speaking What's your favorite meal?

A **PAIR WORK** Add two questions about food to the chart. Then interview your partner. Take notes.

Questions	Name: _____
What's your favorite meal?	
What's your favorite kind of food?	
How often do you have it?	
Who makes it?	
Can you cook it?	
What do you drink with it?	

A: What's your favorite kind of food?

B: I love Mexican food.

B **GROUP WORK** Tell your group about your partner's favorite meal. Do you like that meal, too? Does your group like it?

I can talk about my favorite food. ✓

Wrap-up

1 Quick pair review

Lesson A Brainstorm!

Make a list of count and noncount food words. How many do you know? You have two minutes.

Lesson B Do you remember?

Look at the pictures. Complete the sentences with the correct words. You have one minute.

I ___don't like___ fish ___at all___ .

I _____ French food.

I _____ beef.

I _____ breakfast.

I _____ milk!

I _____ carrots!

Lesson C Find out!

What is one thing both you and your partner eat every week? Eat once in a while?
Never eat? You have two minutes.

A: I eat rice every week. Do you?

B: Yes, I do.

Lesson D Guess!

Describe your favorite food, but don't say its name! Can your partner guess what it is?
Take turns. You have two minutes.

A: I love this food. It's Italian, and I eat it once in a while. I eat it at home.

B: Is it pasta?

A: Yes.

2 In the real world

Go online and find information in English about your favorite movie star's or musician's
eating habits. Then write about them.

- What is his or her favorite food?
- How often does he or she usually eat it?

Bruno Mars's Favorite Food

The American musician Bruno Mars loves
chicken adobo. It's chicken with rice, and it's
the national dish of the Philippines.

8 In the neighborhood

LESSON A	LESSON B	LESSON C	LESSON D
• Places in the neighborhood • Prepositions of location	• Asking for directions	• Places to visit • *There is, there are*	• Reading: "Escape Rooms" • Writing: Group poster

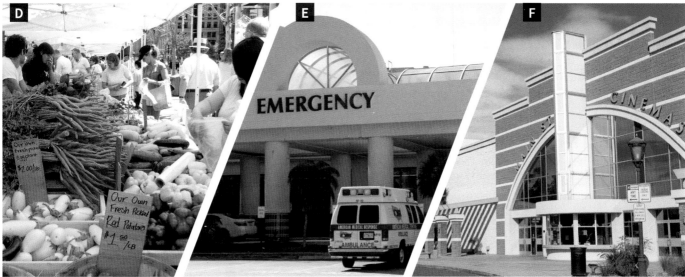

Warm Up

A Look at the pictures. Where can you do these things?

buy flowers	buy some vegetables	find an ATM	eat lunch	see a doctor	see a movie

B What other places can you find in a city?

"You can find a police station."

A Around town

1 Vocabulary Places in the neighborhood

A 🎧 Match the words and the places. Then listen and check (✓) your answers.

a bank	c bus stop	e gas station	g library	i subway station
b bookstore	✓d coffee shop	f hotel	h newsstand	j supermarket

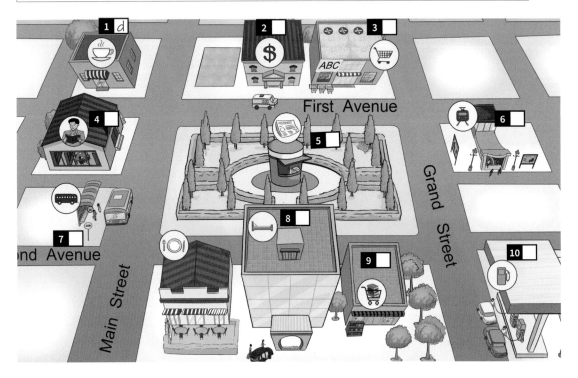

B **PAIR WORK** Which places are in your school's neighborhood?

"We have a coffee shop, some restaurants, and a …"

2 Language in context Ads

A 🎧 Read three advertisements for places in a neighborhood. What places do they describe?

Mama's Place

Come to Mama's Place for real Italian food.

On Second Avenue | 10% off between 5:30 and 6:30 p.m.

Find everything you need at
ABC Supermarket.
New location next to Town Bank

We're always open!

Joe's Coffee Shop

Find us on the
corner of
Main Street and
First Ave.
Best coffee in town!

B What can you do at each place in Part A?

3 Grammar 🎧 Prepositions of location

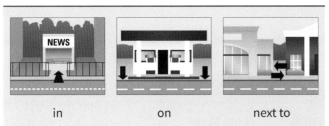

in	on	next to

across from	between	on the corner of

The newsstand is **in** the park.

The gas station is **on** Second Avenue.

The supermarket is **next to** the bank.

The bus stop is **across from** the park.

The hotel is **between** the restaurant and
the bookstore.

The coffee shop is **on the corner of** Main Street
and First Avenue.

Look at the map in Exercise 1. Complete the sentences with the correct prepositions.

1 The newsstand is _____ in _____ the park.

2 The subway station is _____ the park.

3 The bookstore is _____ the hotel.

4 Mama's Place is _____ Second Avenue.

5 The gas station is _____ Second Avenue and Grand Street.

6 The library is _____ the coffee shop and the bus stop.

4 Pronunciation Word stress

🎧 Listen and repeat. Notice the stress
on the first or last syllable.

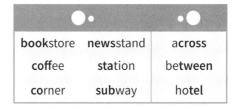

●•	•●
bookstore **news**stand	a**cross**
coffee **sta**tion	be**tween**
corner **sub**way	ho**tel**

5 Speaking Where's the drugstore?

A PAIR WORK Add these four places to the map in Exercise 1. Then ask and answer questions about their locations.

drugstore

post office   police station

department store

A: *Where's the drugstore on your map?*

B: *It's next to the bank. Where is it on your map?*

B PAIR WORK Where are the places in your town? Tell your partner.

6 Keep talking!

Student A go to page 141 and Student B go to page 142 for more practice.

I can give the locations of neighborhood places. ☑

B How do I get to ...?

1 Giving directions

A 🎧 Listen and repeat.

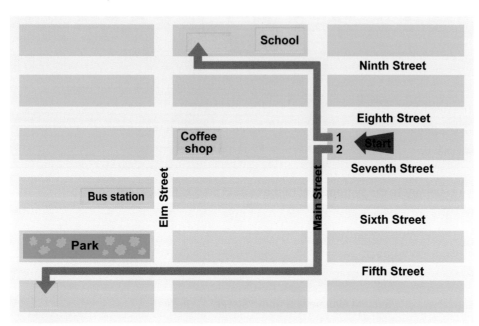

1

Go up Main Street.

Turn left on Ninth Street.

Go one block.

It's **on the right**, next to a school.

2

Walk down Main Street.

Take a right on Fifth Street.

Walk two blocks.

It's **on the left**, across from the park.

B `PAIR WORK` Give directions from *Start* to the coffee shop and the bus station.

2 Interactions Directions

A 🎧 Listen and practice.

Alex   Excuse me. How do I get to the park?

Laura   Go down Seventh Street and take a left on Elm Street. Walk one block to Sixth Street. It's on the right, across from the bus station.

Alex   Turn left on Elm Street?

Laura   Yes.

Alex   Great! Thank you very much.

B 🎧 Listen to the expressions. Then practice the conversation again with the new expression.

Asking for directions

How do I get to ... ?   How can I get to ... ?

3 Listening Follow the route

A 🎧 Listen to Carl and Alice use their GPS to get from Pioneer Square to the library in Seattle. Follow their route. Then mark an X at the library.

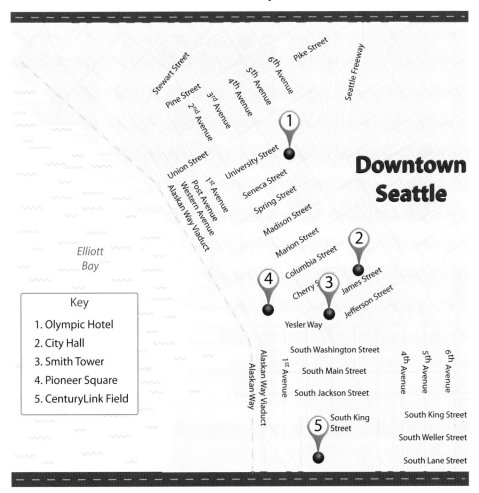

B 🎧 Listen to Carl and Alice go from the library to Pike Place Market. Follow their route. Then mark a ✓ at the market.

C PAIR WORK Give directions from Pioneer Square to other places on the map. Your partner follows them. Take turns.

4 Speaking How do I get to ...?

A PAIR WORK Draw a simple map of the neighborhood around your school. Label different places and street names.

B PAIR WORK Role-play the situation. Then change roles.

Student A: You are a tourist in town. Ask for directions to places in the neighborhood.

Student B: You meet a tourist in your town. Give him or her directions to places in your neighborhood. Start at your school.

A: How do I get to the train station?

B: Walk down Main Street …

I can ask for and give directions. ✓

C Fun in the city

1 Vocabulary Places to visit

A 🎧 Listen and repeat.

amusement park

aquarium

movie theater

museum

science center

swimming pool

water park

zoo

B **PAIR WORK** How often do you go to each place? Tell your partner.

"Our town has a swimming pool, but I hardly ever go there."

2 Conversation Tourist information

🎧 Listen and practice.

Larry Hello. Can I help you?

Maggie Yes. Is there a museum near here?

Larry Let's see … yes. There's a museum across from the park.

Maggie And is there an aquarium in this city?

Larry Yes, there is. It's near the museum. It's a very nice aquarium.

Maggie Great. I have one more question. Are there any amusement parks?

Larry There aren't any amusement parks, but there's a nice water park.

3 Grammar 🎧 *There is, there are*

There's a museum.	**There are** two swimming pools.
There isn't an amusement park.	**There aren't** any good zoos in this city.
Is there an aquarium in this city?	**Are there** any swimming pools near here?
Yes, **there is.** No, **there isn't.**	Yes, **there are.** No, **there aren't.**
Contraction There's = There is	

A Complete the questions about the city with *Is there a / an … ?* or *Are there any … ?* Then compare with a partner.

1 Is there a _____ zoo?
2 _____ water parks?
3 _____ aquarium?
4 _____ museums?
5 _____ amusement park?
6 _____ movie theaters?

B **PAIR WORK** Ask and answer the questions in Part A. Use the map on the right.

A: Is there a zoo?

B: Yes, there is. There's one zoo.

4 Speaking Is there . . . ? Are there . . . ?

A **PAIR WORK** Add two items to the chart. Then interview your partner. Check (✓) the places that are in his or her neighborhood, and ask for more information.

	Places	Locations	Extra information
☐	movie theaters		
☐	museums		
☐	science center		
☐	swimming pool		
☐			
☐			

A: Are there any movie theaters in your neighborhood?

B: Yes, there's one. It's on University Avenue.

A: How often do you go there?

B **CLASS ACTIVITY** Tell the class about two interesting places in your partner's neighborhood.

5 Keep talking!

Go to page 143 for more practice.

I can talk about interesting places in my town. ✓

81

D A great place to visit

1 Reading 🎧

A What are your favorite places to visit?

B Read the article. Where is the world's first escape room?

ESCAPE ROOMS

Imagine! You are in a room with nine other people. Is it a hotel room, an old library, or even a castle? The door is closed, and you can't leave …

Your job: find a key and escape the room. You have only 60 minutes. Is this a movie, a video game, or a bad dream? No – it's an escape room!

Every day, thousands of people visit escape rooms in cities around the world. To find the key and win the game, players answer questions and do puzzles. Players

share information and work in pairs or in groups – you need a team to escape the room!

In some games, there is only one room. In others, you travel through many rooms to escape. Sometimes there are even actors in the room to help you! Some rooms are simple, and most players escape in less than 60 minutes. But some are very difficult, and players hardly ever escape in time.

The world's first escape room is in Japan. But, today, there are more than 2,800 games in many countries.

C Read the article again. Answer the questions.

1 What do players find to escape a room?   _Players find a key._

2 How many people visit escape rooms every day?

3 How long do players have to escape?

4 How do players find the key to the door?

5 Who sometimes help the players?

6 How many escape rooms are there in the world?

D **PAIR WORK** Do you want to visit an escape room? Why or why not? What's another fun adventure that you like?

2 **Listening** City information

A 🎧 Listen to three tourists ask for information about two places in the city.
Write the places in the chart.

	Place 1	Place 2
1	⟨movie theater⟩	
2		
3		

B 🎧 Listen again. Which places are in the city? Circle the correct answers.

3 **Writing and speaking** Group poster presentation

A **GROUP WORK** Choose an interesting place in your city. What do you know about it?
Make a list.

B **GROUP WORK** Create and design a poster about the place. Use your list from Part A.

COME TO THE IMAGINE SCIENCE CENTER! **GREAT FOR KIDS, TEENS, AND ADULTS.**

WE'RE OPEN EVERY DAY FROM 9:00 TO 6:00. • THERE'S A FREE AUDIO TOUR IN TEN LANGUAGES.
THERE'S AN EXCELLENT CAFÉ IN THE MUSEUM. • TRY OUR SCIENCE EXPERIMENTS.
LEARN ABOUT PLANT LIFE. • THERE ARE OVER 10,000 BOOKS IN THE BOOKSTORE.

C **CLASS ACTIVITY** Present your posters. Ask and answer questions for more information.

A: The Imagine Science Center is a great place to visit.

B: It's open every day from 9:00 to 6:00.

C: There's a free audio tour. You can listen to the tour in ten languages.

D: Where is the Imagine Science Center?

C: It's at 367 First Avenue, near the park.

I can give a presentation on a city attraction. ✓

Wrap-up

1 Quick pair review

Lesson A `Brainstorm!`

Make a list of places in a neighborhood. How many do you know? You have one minute.

Lesson B `Do you remember?`

Circle the correct answers. You have two minutes.

A Excuse me. **Where** / (How) do I get to the library from here?

B Walk up Third Avenue and **turn** / **take** left on Elm Street.

A Is the library on Elm Street?

B No, It's not. **Go** / **Turn** two blocks on Elm Street. Then **take** / **walk** a right on Main Street. The library is **on** / **in** the right.

A Thanks!

Lesson C `Find out!`

What are two kinds of places both you and your partner like to visit in your city? What are two kinds of places you don't like to visit? You have two minutes.

A: I like museums. Do you?

B: Not really. How about water parks? I love those!

A: I do, too!

Lesson D `Guess!`

Describe a place to visit in your area, but don't say its name! Can your partner guess the name? Take turns. You have two minutes.

A: I go there with my friends on weekends.

B: Is it Mall Marina?

A: No. There are rides and games there.

B: Is it the amusement park, Fantasy Land?

A: Yes!

2 In the real world

What zoos do you know? Go online and find information in English about a zoo. Then write about it.

- What is the name of the zoo? Where is it?
- What animals and exhibits are there?
- Can you watch videos or take a tour on the website?

The San Diego Zoo

The San Diego Zoo is a famous zoo in California. You can see pandas there. You can also …

9 What are you doing?

Warm Up

A Look at the pictures. Make six sentences about them.

B Which of these things do you do every day?

A I'm looking for you.

1 Vocabulary Actions and prepositions

A 🎧 Listen and repeat.

start

hold

look for

wave

sit

stand

run

end

B 🎧 Listen and repeat.

behind

in

in front of

on

under

C **PAIR WORK** Tell your partner to sit and stand in different places in the classroom.
Use the prepositions. Take turns.

"Stand in front of the door."

2 Language in context Meeting a friend

A 🎧 Listen to Amy and Claudio meet at a soccer game. Where is Amy? Where is Claudio?

Amy   Hi, Claudio. It's Amy. I'm standing under the scoreboard. Where are you?

Claudio   I'm sitting in front of the big clock. Do you see me?

Amy   No, I don't.

Claudio   Well, I'm wearing a red shirt.

Amy   But, Claudio, everyone is wearing a red shirt!

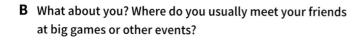

B What about you? Where do you usually meet your friends at big games or other events?

3 Grammar ⌁ Present continuous statements

I'm **standing** under the scoreboard.	I'm **not sitting**.	*Spelling*
You're **running**.	You're **not walking**.	run → run**ning**
He's **sitting** in front of the big clock.	He's **not standing**.	sit → sit**ting**
It's **starting**.	It's **not ending**.	wave → wav**ing**
We're **holding** scarves.	We're **not waving**.	
They're **playing** soccer.	They're **not playing** tennis.	

A Complete Claudio's text messages with the present continuous forms of the verbs.

Where are you, Tim?
I*'m looking* _____ (look) for you.
The game _____
(start), but my favorite player
_____ (not / play) right
now. Please text me.

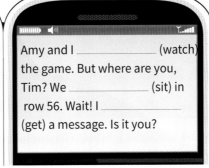

Amy and I _____ (watch)
the game. But where are you,
Tim? We _____ (sit) in
row 56. Wait! I _____
(get) a message. Is it you?

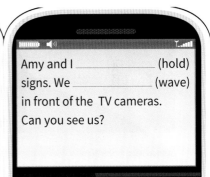

Amy and I _____ (hold)
signs. We _____ (wave)
in front of the TV cameras.
Can you see us?

B **PAIR WORK** Make ten sentences about people in your class with the present continuous.
Tell your partner.

"I'm sitting behind Eva. Lily and Mei are wearing sweaters."

4 Listening Someone is ...

🎧 Listen to the sound effects. What is happening? Circle the correct answers.

1 Someone is (watching a game) / watching a movie.

2 Someone is **getting up** / **going to bed**.

3 Someone is **walking** / **running**.

4 Some people are **playing tennis** /
playing soccer.

5 The game is **starting** / **ending**.

5 Speaking Guess the action.

GROUP WORK Perform an action. Your group guesses it. Take turns.

cook	run	stand
play tennis	sit	watch TV
play the guitar	sleep	wave

A: You're dancing.

B: No, I'm not.

A: You're playing soccer.

B: Yes, that's right.

6 Keep talking!

Go to page 144 for more practice.

Go to page 144 for more practice.

I **can** describe what people are doing right now. ✓

B I can't talk right now.

Interactions Can you talk?

A Look at the pictures. What is Amanda doing?

B 🎧 Listen and practice.

Amanda	Hello?
Justin	Hi, Amanda. It's Justin. Is this a good time to talk?

Amanda	Oh, sorry. I can't talk right now. I'm cooking dinner. Can I call you back?
Justin	OK, sure. Talk to you later.
Amanda	Thanks. Bye.

C 🎧 Listen to the expressions. Then practice the conversation again with the new expressions.

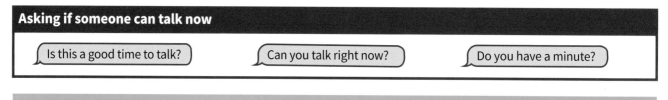

Asking if someone can talk now

| Is this a good time to talk? | Can you talk right now? | Do you have a minute? |

Explaining that you can't talk now

| I can't talk right now. | I'm busy right now. | This isn't a good time. |

D **PAIR WORK** Practice the conversation again with the reasons below.

| clean | do my homework | watch a movie | wait for the doctor |

2 Listening Do you have a minute?

A 🎧 Listen to four phone conversations. Number the questions you hear from 1 to 4.

_____ Can you talk right now? _____ Is this a good time to talk?

_____ Is this a good time? __1__ Do you have a minute?

B 🎧 Listen again. Why can't each person talk right now? Write the reason.

1 Eric __is having dinner__ . 3 Ji-won _____ .

2 Renee _____ . 4 Carmen _____ .

3 Speaking Role play

A Complete the sentences with reasons why you can't talk on the phone.

I'm watching _____ . I'm eating _____ .

I'm studying _____ . I'm _____ .

B **PAIR WORK** Role-play the situations. Then change roles.

Student A: Answer the phone. Explain that you can't talk now and say why. Use the reasons from part A.

Student B: Call Student A. Identify yourself and ask if he or she can talk right now.

I can ask if someone can talk now. ✓

I can explain why I can't talk on the telephone. ✓

C These days

1 Vocabulary Activities

A 🎧 Listen and repeat.

create a website

learn to drive

look for a job

study for an exam

study Italian

take a dance class

take tennis lessons

tutor a student

B **PAIR WORK** Which activities are fun? Which are not fun? Compare answers with a partner.

2 Conversation Old friends

🎧 Listen and practice.

Jill	Long time no see, Wendy!
Wendy	Oh, hi, Jill!
Jill	What are you doing these days?
Wendy	I'm learning to drive. I'm also tutoring a student. Oh, and I'm taking a dance class.
Jill	You sound really busy.
Wendy	I am. How about you, Jill? Are *you* doing anything special these days?
Jill	Yes, I am. I'm studying Italian.
Wendy	Really? Why are you studying Italian?
Jill	Because ... Oh, my phone is ringing. Hello? Sorry, Wendy. It's my new friend, Luigi.
Wendy	Oh.
Jill	*Ciao, Luigi! Come stai?*

3 Grammar 🎧 Present continuous questions

What **are** you **doing** these days?
    I**'m learning** to drive.
 	
What class **is** Wendy **taking**?
    She**'s taking** a dance class.
 	
Where **are** they **studying**?
    They**'re studying** online.
	Are you **doing** anything special these days?
	    Yes, I **am**. No, I**'m not**.
	
	Is she **tutoring** a student?
	    Yes, she **is**. No, she**'s not**.
	
	Are they **taking** tennis lessons?
	    Yes, they **are**. No, they**'re not**.

A Complete the questions with the present continuous forms of the verbs. Then compare with a partner.

1   _____Are_____ you _____taking_____ (take) music lessons these days?

2   What classes _____ you _____ (take)?

3   _____ you and your friends _____ (buy) new music these days?

4   What _____ your classmates _____ (learn) in this class?

5   What languages _____ you _____ (study)?

6   _____ you _____ (learn) to drive?

B **PAIR WORK** Ask and answer the questions in Part A. Answer with your own information.

4 Pronunciation Intonation in questions

🎧 Listen and repeat. Notice the intonation of *yes / no* and *Wh-* questions.

Are you watching a lot of TV?   What TV shows are you watching?

5 Speaking Busy lives

CLASS ACTIVITY Add two activities to the chart. Then find classmates who are doing each thing these days. Write their names and ask questions for more information.

Are you … these days?	Name	Extra information
studying another language		
reading a good book		
watching a lot of TV		
taking any fun classes		
streaming a lot of music		

6 Keep talking!

Go to page 145 for more practice.

I can describe what people are doing these days. ✓

D What's new?

1 Reading 🎧

A What are you and your classmates doing right now?

B Read the status updates. Which two people are waiting for other people?

WHAT'S YOUR STATUS?   🔍   SIGN UP   LOGIN

Type your message here and hit enter

Donna Bristol   I'm standing under the JB Cola sign on Main Street. I'm waiting for my friend Hank. But Hank is never late! Hank?
APR 19 8:33 P.M.

Hank Jones   I'm standing in line. Donna, please wait!! I'm in a store on First Avenue. The line isn't moving.
APR 19 8:50 P.M.

Fernando Sanchez   I'm studying English. I'm doing grammar exercises online. I'm getting them all correct. Yay!
APR 19 9:05 P.M.

Zack Parker   I'm enjoying Singapore!! I love vacations! How are my friends in Chicago doing?
APR 19 9:17 P.M.

Hee-jin Park   I'm having a great evening. I'm at my favorite restaurant with my two friends, Alex and Eddie. We're waiting for dessert.
APR 19 9:28 P.M.

Jessica King   I'm looking for a good French dictionary. I'm taking a French class and need help with my vocabulary.
APR 19 9:44 P.M.

Arthur Henderson   I'm waiting for my daughter to come home. It's almost 10:00 p.m. Where are you, Lisa? You know the rules!
APR 19 9:58 P.M.

Lisa Henderson   I'm at a basketball game. Sorry, Dad. My favorite player is playing. 15 more minutes?
APR 19 10:02 P.M.

C Read the updates again. Complete the sentences with first names.

1 _____Zack_____ is on vacation.
2 _____ is having dinner.
3 _____ is standing in line.
4 _____ is watching a basketball game.
5 _____ and _____ are students.
6 _____ and _____ are late.

D **PAIR WORK** How often do you write messages like the ones above? What do you write about? Tell your partner.

"I love status updates. I write them twice a day. I usually write about the new music I find online."

92

2 **Writing** My status update

A Write or tell your classmates in a group chat what you're doing right now or these days.

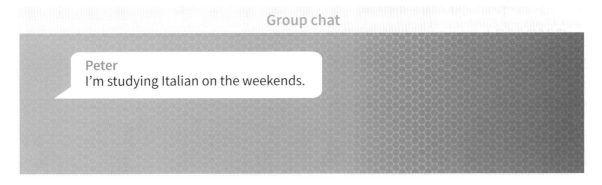

Group chat

> **Peter**
> I'm studying Italian on the weekends.

B GROUP WORK Pass your paper to the classmate on your right or send an update to the group. Read and respond to your classmate's update. Continue to pass, read, and respond to each classmate's update three times with different actions.

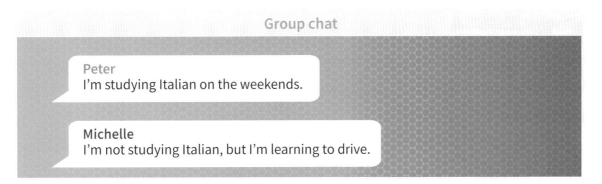

Group chat

> **Peter**
> I'm studying Italian on the weekends.

> **Michelle**
> I'm not studying Italian, but I'm learning to drive.

3 **Speaking** Makoto's Desk

GROUP WORK Look at Makoto's desk. What do you think he's doing these days?

A: I think he's studying French.

B: Right. And he's playing tennis.

C: Do you think he's drinking a lot of coffee?

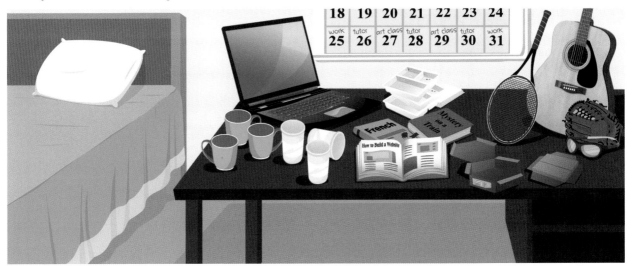

I can discuss what people are doing. ✓

Wrap-up

1 Quick pair review

Lesson A Do you remember?

Complete the sentences with the correct prepositions. You have one minute.

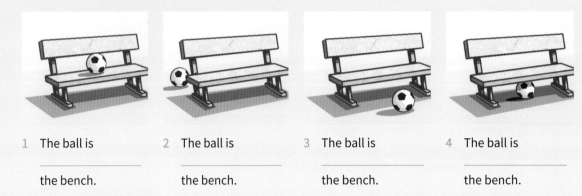

1 The ball is
_____
the bench.

2 The ball is
_____
the bench.

3 The ball is
_____
the bench.

4 The ball is
_____
the bench.

Lesson B Brainstorm!

Make a list of phone expressions. How many do you know? You have two minutes.

Lesson C Find out!

What are two things both you and your partner are doing these days? You have one minute.

A: What are you doing these days?

B: I'm taking tango lessons. Are you?

A: No, I'm not.

Lesson D Guess!

Describe the clothes and actions of someone in your class, but don't say his or her name!
Can your partner guess the name? Take turns. You have two minutes.

A: He's wearing a baseball cap and talking to Angela right now.

B: Is it Sebastian?

A: Yes, it is.

2 In the real world

Go to a mall or park. What are people doing? Write about them.

People in the Park

I am in the park. Two women are walking. One woman is wearing a red T-shirt. A man is sitting next to me. He is eating his lunch. He is also ...

10 Past experiences

A — Benjamin, age 16

B — Benjamin, age 43

C — Luz, age 14

D — Luz, age 29

Warm Up

A Look at the pictures. Make three sentences about each one.

B How are *you* different now?

A Last weekend

1 Vocabulary Weekend activities

A 🎧 Listen and repeat.

listen to music

play basketball

play in a band

shop for new clothes

stay home

stay out late

visit relatives

watch an old movie

B **PAIR WORK** Do you do any of the activities in Part A? When do you do them? Tell your partner.

"My friends and I usually play basketball on Saturday mornings."

2 Language in context Carmen's weekend

A 🎧 Listen to Carmen talk about last weekend. Number the pictures from 1 to 3.

1 Last Saturday morning, my brother Pedro called me. We talked for hours. I uploaded some photos, and I listened to music.

2 I stayed out late on Saturday night. Pedro and I watched an old movie. We laughed a lot. We loved it!

3 On Sunday afternoon, I stayed home. I watched another movie. I didn't like the ending at all. I cried.

1

B What about you? What do you usually do on weekends?

3 Grammar 🎧 Simple past regular verbs

I **listened** to music last Saturday. You **stayed** home. He **called** me on Saturday. We **laughed**. They **stayed** out late.	I **didn't watch** a movie. You **didn't stay** out late. He **didn't call** me on Sunday. We **didn't cry**. They **didn't stay** at home.	*Spelling* stay → stay**ed** love → lov**ed** cry → cr**ied** shop → shop**ped**

A Write sentences about the things Pedro did and didn't do last weekend.

Things to Do

✓ call Carmen   ✗ listen to music

✓ watch a movie   ✓ upload photos

✗ play basketball   ✗ shop for new clothes

1 Pedro called Carmen.
2 _____
3 _____
4 _____
5 _____
6 _____

B **PAIR WORK** Make true sentences about your weekend with the past forms of the verbs in Part A. Tell your partner.

4 Pronunciation Simple past *-ed* endings

A 🎧 Listen and repeat. Notice that some verbs have an extra syllable in the past tense.

Same syllable (most verbs)		Extra syllable (verbs ending in *t* and *d*)	
call / called		chat / chat·ted	
listen / listened		start / start·ed	
play / played		upload / upload·ed	

B 🎧 Listen. Complete the chart with the correct verbs.

download / downloaded post / posted	shop / shopped stay / stayed	visit / visited watch / watched

5 Speaking A fun weekend

A Complete the phrases with your own ideas.

chat with _____   exercise _____   study _____   visit _____

cook _____   look for _____   talk to _____   walk to _____

B **PAIR WORK** Tell your partner about the things you did and didn't do last weekend. Use the phrases from Part A to help you.

A: I chatted online with my friends last weekend. How about you?

B: I didn't chat online with my friends, but I called them.

6 Keep talking!

Go to page 146 for more practice.

I can say what I did last weekend. ✓

B You're kidding!

1 Interactions Expressing surprise

A Look at the pictures. What do you think Diego and Jasmine are talking about?

B 🎧 Listen and practice.

Diego I checked plane tickets to go to Walt Disney World in May.

Jasmine Uh-huh.

Diego They're usually $600, but right now they're $350!

Jasmine You're kidding!

Diego I know. I didn't buy them, but I called my parents, and they liked the idea.

Jasmine That's great. I love that place.

C 🎧 Listen to the expressions. Then practice the conversation again with the new expressions.

Showing that you're listening		
Uh-huh.	Oh?	Oh, yeah?

Expressing surprise		
Really?	What?	You're kidding!

D **PAIR WORK** Check (✓) the best responses. Then practice with a partner.

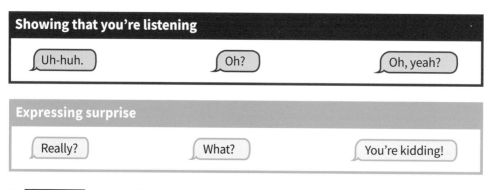

1 I watched a movie last night.   ✓ Uh-huh.   ☐ Really?

2 I listened to 500 songs yesterday.   ☐ You're kidding!   ☐ Oh?

3 I didn't study for the big test.   ☐ Oh, yeah?   ☐ What?

4 I played tennis with friends on Sunday. ☐ You're kidding!   ☐ Oh, yeah?

98

2 Listening What a week!

A 🎧 Listen to Diana tell her friend about the past week. Number the pictures from 1 to 4.

B 🎧 Listen again. What surprises Diana's friend? Complete the sentences.

1 Diana didn't ____answer____ three ____questions____.

2 Diana's _____ boyfriend _____ her.

3 Julie didn't _____ the _____.

4 Diana _____ home on _____.

3 Speaking Really?

A Match the sentences. Then compare with a partner.

1 Last night, I studied for my English test for five hours. _b_

2 I just checked my email. ____

3 Last week, I streamed two movies. ____

4 On Thursday, I started a new class. ____

a I watched them with my dad.

b But I didn't get a good score.

c I'm learning Chinese.

d I have 100 new messages.

B PAIR WORK Role-play the situations in Part A. Then change roles.

Student A: Say the lines from Part A.

Student B: Show interest or express surprise.

A: Last night, I studied for my English test for five hours, but I didn't get a good score.

B: You're kidding! Why not?

C PAIR WORK Role-play new situations. Use your own ideas.

I can show that I'm listening. ✓
I can express surprise. ✓

99

C Did you make dinner last night?

1 Vocabulary Things to do

A 🎧 Listen and repeat.

do laundry

do the dishes

get a haircut

go grocery shopping

have a party

make dinner

see a play

see friends

sleep

B **PAIR WORK** How often do you do the things in Part A? Tell your partner.

"I *do* laundry *once a week*. I *do* the dishes *every day* ..."

2 Conversation Last night

🎧 Listen and practice.

Mindy   Hi, Pete. Did you see Jennifer last night?

Pete   Yes, I did. But the day didn't go so well.

Mindy   Really? What happened?

Pete   Well, I did my laundry yesterday morning, but my favorite white shirt turned pink.

Mindy   You're kidding!

Pete   Then I got a haircut, but I really didn't like it.

Mindy   Oh, yeah? Did you make dinner for Jennifer?

Pete   Well, I slept for a while, so I didn't go grocery shopping.

Mindy   Oh. Did you eat anything?

Pete   Yeah, we did. Jennifer bought a pizza for us.

Mindy   Really?

3 Grammar 🎧 Simple past irregular verbs; *yes* / *no* questions

I **saw** Jennifer last night.
She **bought** a pizza.
They **ate** a pizza.

I **didn't see** Jennifer last week.
She **didn't buy** soup.
They **didn't eat** salad.

Did you **see** Jennifer last night?
　Yes, I **did**.　　No, I **didn't**.
Did she **buy** dinner?
　Yes, she **did**.　　No, she **didn't**.
Did they **eat** dinner?
　Yes, they **did**.　　No, they **didn't**.

A Complete the conversation with the simple past tense form of the verbs. Then practice with a partner.

A　Hey, Pablo. ___Did___ you ___do___ (do) today's homework?

B　I _____ . I _____ (not / have) time.

A　Really? Why not?

B　I _____ (see) some friends yesterday. We _____ (eat) lunch, and then we _____ (go) to the mall.

A　Oh, yeah? _____ you _____ (buy) any clothes?

B　I _____ (not / buy) anything! So, _____ you _____ (do) *your* homework?

A　Yes, I did. And no, you can't see it!

> 🎧 **Common irregular verbs**
> buy → **bought**　　have → **had**
> do → **did**　　make → **made**
> drink → **drank**　　meet → **met**
> drive → **drove**　　read → **read**
> eat → **ate**　　see → **saw**
> fall → **fell**　　sleep → **slept**
> get → **got**　　take → **took**
> go → **went**　　write → **wrote**
>
> *Go to page 152 for a list of more irregular verbs.*

B Put the words in order to make questions. Then compare with a partner.

1　last night / you / see / did / your friends　　_Did you see your friends last night?_

2　go / last weekend / you / did / grocery shopping

3　watch / you / a movie / did / last night

4　yesterday / stay home / you / did

5　make dinner / did / on Thursday / you

6　you / did / last Saturday / have a party

C **PAIR WORK** Ask and answer the questions in Part B. Answer with your own information.

A: Did you see your friends last night?

B: Yes, I did. I saw two friends. We ate out at a restaurant.

4 Speaking Did you?

A **PAIR WORK** Add two past time expressions to the list. Then ask and answer *Did you ... ?* questions with each time expression. Take notes.

A: Did you make dinner last night?

B: Yes, I did. Did you do laundry last night?

A: No, I didn't.

Past time expressions	
last night	last week
yesterday	last weekend

B **GROUP WORK** Tell your group about your partner's answers. Did anyone do anything interesting?

5 Keep talking!

Go to page 147 for more practice.

I can talk about routine events in the past. ☑

D I saw a great movie.

1 Reading

A Do you read the review of a movie before you watch it? Or do you think it spoils the fun?

B Read Matt's review and the comments people made. Who liked the movie?

Matt's Movie Reviews

HOME   REVIEWS   CONTACT ME

Too Young to Love

On Friday, my friend Naomi and I hung out together. We had a very good time. We saw a great old movie at the Cineplex. They are showing old movies all month. Did anyone see *Too Young to Love*? I loved it! It's a story about two young people who are in love. Their parents think they are too young, so they can't get married. It's not a sad movie. It's really funny! We laughed a lot.
MONDAY, 11:00

CGIRL   I saw *Too Young to Love*. I also saw the play. Both are good. See the movie and the play.
MONDAY, 11:26 A.M

OSCAR   *Too Young to Love*?! You're kidding! I hated the movie, but I liked the music. The sound track had some really good old songs. MONDAY, 1:00 P.M.

TOMAS   My friend and I saw it. She laughed. I cried because I paid for the tickets, and I didn't like it at all. TUESDAY, 7:00 A.M.

JOE C   I liked *Too Young to Love*. I saw three old movies at the Cineplex last month, and I really liked all of them. TUESDAY, 12:45 P.M.

MARIA   What?! *Too Young to Love*?! I hated the movie, but I loved the book. TUESDAY, 1:15 P.M.

C Read the blog again. Correct the false sentences.

1 Matt saw the movie on ~~Saturday~~.   *Matt saw the movie on Friday.*

2 Oscar hated the music.

3 Tomas liked *Too Young to Love*.

4 Joe C didn't see any movies at the Cineplex last month.

5 Maria hated the book *Too Young to Love*.

D PAIR WORK Do you or your friends ever post reviews of movies, food, or places you visit online? What do you post about? Tell your partner.

"My friend Rosa reviews every restaurant she goes to. She is a hard critic!"

2 Writing A blog post

A Choose one day last week. Complete the chart with information about the things you did that day.

Day	Activities	Places	Other information

B Write a blog post about that day. Use the model and your answers in Part A to help.

C **PAIR WORK** Share your post. Ask and answer questions for more information.

"Did you have a good time? Did you eat out?"

> ### Friday
>
> After class, I met my friend Terry. We went shopping at the mall. I bought a new watch. I didn't pay much for it, but I really like it. I went home at 8:00 p.m.

3 Listening A busy week

A 🎧 Listen to Matt talk about last week. What activities did he do? Check (✓) the correct answers.

- ☐ did laundry
- ☑ got up early
- ☐ got up late
- ☐ made dinner
- ☐ played soccer
- ☐ played the guitar
- ☐ read books
- ☐ stayed out late
- ☐ worked

B 🎧 Listen again. What activities did Matt enjoy? Circle the activities above.

4 Speaking I played in a band last year.

A **CLASS ACTIVITY** Add two past activities to the chart. Then find classmates who did each thing. Write their names and ask questions for more information.

Find someone who ...	Name	Extra information
bought a cell phone last year		
got a haircut last week		
saw a friend yesterday		
made dinner last night		
watched a game on TV last weekend		
wrote a blog post yesterday		

A: Did you buy a cell phone last year, Alex?
B: Yes, I did.

B **GROUP WORK** Share your information.

"Alex bought a cell phone last year."

I can talk about past activities. ✓

Wrap-up

1 Quick pair review

Lesson A **Find out!**

What are three things both you and your partner did after class yesterday?
What are three things you didn't do? You have two minutes.

A: I walked home after class yesterday. Did you?

B: Yes, I did. I watched TV at home. Did you?

A: No, I didn't. I listened to music.

Lesson B **Do you remember?**

Circle the correct answers. You have two minutes.

1 A   I listened to all of Taylor Swift's songs today.

   B   **Oh? /** *You're kidding!* *All* of them?
      She has a lot!

2 A   Janet uploaded photos from the party.

   B   **Uh-huh. / Really?** I know. I looked at them
      this morning.

3 A   Charlie's band played at The Red Room
      downtown on Saturday night!

   B   **What? / Oh?** No way! That's so cool!
      I didn't know that.

4 A   I visited my grandmother last weekend.

   B   **You're kidding! / Oh, yeah?** How is she doing?

Lesson C **Test your partner!**

Say eight irregular verbs in the simple present. Can your partner write the simple past forms
of the verbs correctly? Check his or her answers. You have two minutes.

1 _____   3 _____   5 _____   7 _____

2 _____   4 _____   6 _____   8 _____

Lesson D **Guess!**

Make two true sentences and one false sentence about your activities last week. Can your
partner guess the false sentence? Take turns. You have two minutes.

A: I watched 20 movies last week. I played basketball in the park. I saw a play.

B: You didn't watch 20 movies.

A: You're right. I only watched 12.

2 In the real world

Did anyone else do the same things as you yesterday? Go online and find three English-speaking
bloggers who did the same activities as you yesterday. Then write about them.

- What activities did both you and the bloggers do yesterday?
- What are the bloggers' names? Where are they from?

Bloggers and Me

I played basketball yesterday. Three bloggers also played basketball yesterday.
Diego is from California. He played basketball with his brother.

11 Getting away

LESSON A	LESSON B	LESSON C	LESSON D
● Adjectives ● Past of *be*	● Reacting to good news ● Reacting to bad news	● Vacation activities ● Simple past *Wh-* questions	● Reading: "Travel Tales" ● Writing: A postcard

Warm Up

A Do you know any of these places? Which ones?

B What are some popular places to visit in your country? In your city?

A Where were you?

1 Vocabulary Adjectives

A 🎧 Listen and repeat.

exciting / fun / great

all right / OK / so-so

awful / terrible

boring

interesting

noisy

quiet

B **PAIR WORK** Think of things that each adjective describes. Discuss your ideas.

A: Sports are exciting.

B: Basketball is exciting, but I think soccer is boring.

2 Language in context Quick getaways

A 🎧 Listen to four people talk about recent trips. Number the pictures from 1 to 4.

1 We went on a school trip last week. We went to a theater and saw an exciting play. The actors were great.

–Olivia

2 We just had a three-day weekend. I went away with my family. It was a fun trip, but our hotel wasn't very nice. In fact, it was terrible.

–Ichiro

3 I was at my brother's apartment last weekend. He doesn't have a TV or a computer. It was quiet and kind of boring.

–Brian

4 My friend and I went on a day trip last week. We took a local bus to an old town. The bus was awful and noisy, but the trip was interesting. Look what I bought!

–Eleanor

1

B Did each person like his or her trip? Why or why not?

3 Grammar 🎧 Past of *be*

Where were you last weekend? I **was** at my brother's apartment. **How was** your weekend? It **was** quiet and kind of boring. *I / he / she / it* *you / we / they* **was** **were**	**Was** your trip interesting? Yes, it **was**. No, it **wasn't**. **Were** the people nice? Yes, they **were**. No, they **weren't**. *Contractions* wasn't = was not weren't = were not

A Complete the guest comment card with *was*, *were*, *wasn't*, or *weren't*. Then compare with a partner.

Guest comments

My wife, son, and I _____*were*_____ guests at your hotel last week. Unfortunately, we _____ happy with our

room. The room _____ clean, and the beds _____ awful. And the room _____ near the

street. The noise _____ terrible in the early morning. But the people at the hotel _____ great, so

that _____ good!

B Read the answers. Write the questions. Then practice with a partner.

1. How was your weekend? _____ It was great.
2. _____ Yes, my weekend was interesting.
3. _____ I was on a trip.
4. _____ No, I wasn't at the theater on Friday.
5. _____ Yes, I was at home on Sunday afternoon.
6. _____ My parents were in Tahiti.

C **PAIR WORK** Ask and answer the questions in Part B. Answer with your own information.

4 Speaking Where were you last Friday night?

A **PAIR WORK** Interview your partner. Take notes.

Where were you ... ?	Location	Extra information
at this time yesterday		
on your birthday		
on New Year's Eve		
last Friday night		

B **GROUP WORK** Tell your group about your partner's answers. Who was in an interesting place? Who did interesting things?

5 Keep talking!

Go to page 148 for more practice.

I can describe where I was in the past. ✓

B That's great!

1 Good news, bad news

A 🎧 Listen and repeat.

I got a promotion.   I lost my wallet.   I missed my flight.   I was sick.   I won a contest.

B **PAIR WORK** Which things are good news? Which are bad news? Can you think of other examples? Discuss your ideas.

2 Interactions Reacting to news

A 🎧 Listen and practice.

Meg Did you have a good weekend?	**Joe** And how was your weekend?
Joe Yes! It was my sister's birthday, so we went to the beach.	**Meg** It wasn't so good. I lost my phone.
Meg Really? That's great!	**Joe** Oh, no! What happened?

B 🎧 Listen to the expressions. Then practice the conversation again with the new expressions.

Reacting to good news

That's great!   That's excellent!   That's awesome!

Reacting to bad news

Oh, no!   That's too bad.   That's terrible!

C **PAIR WORK** Practice the conversation again with the examples from Exercise 1. React to the news.

A: Did you have a good weekend?

B: Yes! I got a promotion, so I went shopping.

108

3 Listening A short trip

A 🎧 Listen to Sam tell a friend about a short trip. Number the pictures from 1 to 6.

B 🎧 Listen again. Was Sam's trip great, good, bad, or awful?

4 Speaking That's ... !

A Write three good things and three bad things that happened to you last week.

	Good things that happened	Bad things that happened
1		
2		
3		

B **CLASS ACTIVITY** Ask your classmates about their week. React to the news.

A: Did you do anything interesting last week?

B: Well, I started a new job.

A: That's excellent!

B: Yeah. But I lost my cell phone.

A: That's terrible!

I can react to news. ✓

C My vacation

1 Vocabulary Vacation activities

A 🎧 Listen and repeat.

buy souvenirs

go sightseeing

go to a festival

go to the beach

relax

shop in markets

take a tour

take pictures

B **PAIR WORK** Did you do any of the activities in Part A on your last vacation? Tell your partner.

"On my last vacation, I bought souvenirs and took pictures. I didn't go to the beach."

2 Conversation Back from vacation

🎧 Listen and practice.

Dave How was your vacation, Kate?

Kate Oh, it was exciting. We had a great time.

Dave Where did you go?

Kate I went to Veracruz, Mexico.

Dave That's great. Who did you travel with?

Kate My sister.

Dave When did you get back?

Kate Last night. I got home at midnight.

Dave Really? That's late! So, what did you do there?

Kate Well, we went to a festival called *Carnaval*. We also shopped in local markets and took lots of pictures. Look, I bought you a souvenir.

Dave Thanks! I love it!

3 Grammar 🎧 Simple past *Wh-* questions

Where did you **go** on vacation?
  I went to Veracruz, Mexico.
 	
When did you **get** back?
  Last night.
 	
Who did you **travel** with?
  My sister.
	What did you **do** there?
	  We went to a festival and shopped.
	
	Why did you **go** to Veracruz?
	  Because the festival is famous.
	
	How did you **get** to Veracruz?
	  By plane.

Match the questions and the answers. Then practice with a partner.

1 Where did you go on vacation? __f__
2 Who did you go with? _____
3 When did you get back? _____
4 What did you do on vacation? _____
5 Why did you go to Vietnam? _____
6 How did you travel in Vietnam? _____

a We got back last week.
b We took the bus and the train.
c We relaxed and took pictures.
d Because I have friends there.
e I went with my brother.
f I went to Vietnam.

4 Pronunciation Reduction of *did you*

A 🎧 **Listen and repeat. Notice how** *did you* **is pronounced /dɪdʒə/ after** *Wh-* **question words.**

  Where **did you** go?   What **did you** do?   When **did you** get back?

B **PAIR WORK** Practice the questions in the grammar chart. Reduce *did you* to /dɪdʒə/ after *Wh-* question words.

5 Speaking What a vacation!

A Answer the questions.

● Where did you go on your last vacation? _____
● Who did you go with? _____
● When did you go? _____
● What did you do there? _____
● How did you travel? _____
● Did you buy anything? _____
● What did you like about the vacation? _____
● What didn't you like about the vacation? _____

fly → flew

B **GROUP WORK** Tell your group about your last vacation. Ask and answer questions for more information.

6 Keep talking!

Go to page 149 for more practice.

take a boat → took a boat

I can talk about my last vacation. ✅

1 Reading 🎧

A How often do you go on vacation? Where do you go?

B Read the travel blog posts. What country is each person visiting?

TRAVEL TALES

I'm here in Chiang Mai, Thailand. Yesterday, I went on a short elephant ride. There was a man on the elephant in front of me. His name was Alan Johnson. My name is Alan Johnson, too!
POSTED ON OCTOBER 12, 10:30 A.M.
ALAN JOHNSON

My sister and I are in Paris, France. It's our first trip overseas. We went to an outdoor café the other day, and Johnny Depp was at the next table. How exciting!
POSTED ON OCTOBER 14, 6:48 P.M.
MARY O'CONNOR

I'm here with my parents at a hotel in Miami, Florida. We came to visit our relatives. We all went to bed last night at about midnight. At 3:00 in the morning, we heard a fire alarm.
POSTED ON OCTOBER 15, 8:06 A.M.
ANITA GONZALEZ

I'm in Granada, Nicaragua. I came here to help build houses. It's a great country. We finished our first house yesterday. We're not staying in a hotel. We're staying in a school.
POSTED ON OCTOBER 21, 9:12 P.M.
DIANE NICHOLSON

C Read the blog posts again. What is the last sentence of each post? Number the posts from 1 to 4.

1 Last night, we all slept in one big room!

2 He was nice to us, and I have a cool photo now.

3 I can't believe that we have the same name!

4 We ran down to the street and were fine.

D **PAIR WORK** What adjectives describe each travel experience? Discuss your ideas.

A: I think Alan Johnson's trip was very exciting!

B: Me, too. I love elephants, and Thailand is an interesting country.

2 **Listening** Three different trips

A 🎧 Listen to three people talk about their vacations. How do they describe them? Check (✓) the correct answers.

	How were their vacations?		What was one thing they liked?
1	☐ awful	✓ great	shopping
	☐ boring	☐ so-so	
2	☐ fun	☐ OK	
	☐ interesting	☐ terrible	
3	☐ awful	☐ exciting	
	☐ boring	☐ great	

B 🎧 Listen again. What did they like about their trips? Write one thing for each person in the chart.

3 **Writing and speaking** A postcard

A Read Sofia's postcard to Jack about her vacation.

Dear Jack,

Linda and I are having a great time here in Morocco. We took a train from Casablanca to Marrakech yesterday. Last night, we went to a big "souk," or market. We walked around the market for hours! I bought a nice souvenir for you.

See you soon!
Sofia

B Write a postcard to a friend or family member about an experience you had on vacation. Use the model in Part A to help you.

C CLASS ACTIVITY Post your postcards around the room. Read your classmates' postcards. Then write questions about five postcards that interest you.

1. Eddie – What did you buy for your sister?

2. Jung-woo – Who did you travel with?

3. Marcus – When did you take this vacation?

D CLASS ACTIVITY Find the classmates who wrote the five postcards. Ask them your questions.

A: Eddie, what did you buy your sister?

B: I bought a scarf.

A: I see, thanks. Excuse me, Jung-woo, who did you travel with?

I can describe a vacation. ✓

Wrap-up

1 Quick pair review

Lesson A `Brainstorm!`

Make a list of adjectives. How many do you know? You have one minute.

Lesson B `Do you remember?`

Check (✓) the correct answers. You have one minute.

1 I won a free ticket to Jamaica. ☑ That's great! ☐ Oh, no!
2 I lost my cell phone. ☐ That's terrible! ☐ That's excellent!
3 My sister missed her flight. ☐ That's awesome. ☐ That's too bad.
4 Charlie met Leonardo DiCaprio. ☐ Oh, no! ☐ That's great!

Lesson C `Find out!`

What are two things both you and your partner did on your last vacation?
You have two minutes.

A: Did you go sightseeing on your last vacation?

B: Yes, I did. How about you?

A: Yes, I went sightseeing, too.

Lesson D `Test your partner!`

Describe a vacation. Can your partner draw a postcard of your vacation?
Check his or her drawing. You have two minutes.

"Last year, my sister and I went to Madrid, Spain.
We shopped in El Rastro Market and went to
art museums."

2 In the real world

Do you ever read travel blogs? Go online and find
a travel blog in English. Then write about it.

- Where did the blogger go?
- When did he or she go there?
- What did he or she do there?

Kelly's Travel Blog

Kelly is a blogger from Canada. Last week, she
went on vacation to Scotland. She went
sightseeing in Glasgow. She went to ...

12 Time to celebrate

wedding

Warm Up

A Label the pictures with the correct words.

| birthday | graduation | holiday | ✓ wedding |

B What special events do you celebrate?

A I'm going to get married.

1 Vocabulary Months and dates

A 🎧 Listen and repeat.

January	February	March	April	May	June
July	August	September	October	November	December

1st first	**9th** ninth	**17th** seventeenth	**25th** twenty-fifth
2nd second	**10th** tenth	**18th** eighteenth	**26th** twenty-sixth
3rd third	**11th** eleventh	**19th** nineteenth	**27th** twenty-seventh
4th fourth	**12th** twelfth	**20th** twentieth	**28th** twenty-eighth
5th fifth	**13th** thirteenth	**21st** twenty-first	**29th** twenty-ninth
6th sixth	**14th** fourteenth	**22nd** twenty-second	**30th** thirtieth
7th seventh	**15th** fifteenth	**23rd** twenty-third	**31st** thirty-first
8th eighth	**16th** sixteenth	**24th** twenty-fourth	

B **CLASS ACTIVITY** **When is your birthday? Stand in the order of your birthdays, from the first to the last in the year.**

A: My birthday is July twenty-eighth.

B: Mine is July twentieth. You're next to me.

2 Language in context Special days

A 🎧 **Listen to three people talk about special days. What are the dates of the special days?**

I'm going to graduate from high school on June 8th. I'm going to start college in September.
–Sarah

My eightieth birthday is on August 21st. I'm going to go skydiving for the first time. I can't wait!
–Walter

My boyfriend, Kenta, and I are going to get married on October 16th. We're going to have a big wedding.
–Mari

B **What about you? What days of the year are special to you? Why?**

3 Grammar 🎧 *Be going to; yes / no* questions

I'm **going to graduate** on June 8th.	**Are** you **going to start** college?
I'm **not going to start** college in July.	Yes, I am. No, I'm not.
Walter**'s going to go** skydiving.	**Is** Walter **going to go** skydiving?
He**'s not going to play** basketball.	Yes, he is. No, he isn't.
Mari and Kenta **are going to get** married.	**Are** they **going to have** a big wedding?
They**'re not going to have** a small wedding.	Yes, they are. No, they aren't.

A Complete the conversation with the correct forms of *be going to.*
Then practice with a partner.

A   _____Are_____ you ___going to graduate___ (graduate)
from college this year?

B   Yeah, on May 30th. My parents _____ (have)
a big party for me.

A   Great! _____ the party _____ (be)
at their house?

B   No, it _____ (not / be) at the house.
They _____ (have) it at a restaurant.

A   _____ you _____ (get) a job right away?

B   No, I'm not. First, I _____ (travel).
Then I _____ (look) for a job.

B **PAIR WORK** Ask and answer three *Are you going to … ?* questions.
Answer with your own information.

4 Pronunciation Reduction of *going to* before verbs

A 🎧 Listen and repeat. Notice how *going to* is reduced to /gənə/ in informal
spoken English.

Are you **going to** do anything special?   Yes. I'm **going to** go skydiving.

B **PAIR WORK** Practice the sentences in the grammar chart. Reduce *going to*
to /gənə/.

5 Speaking Three special days

A Write the dates and your plans for three special days or holidays next year.

	Special day: _____	Special day: _____	Special day: _____
Dates			
Plans			

B **PAIR WORK** Tell your partner about your special days. Ask and answer questions for more information.

6 Keep talking!

Go to page 150 for more practice.

I can talk about my plans for specific dates. ✓

B Sure. I'd love to.

1 Interactions Invitations

A How often do you go to the movies with your friends?

B 🎧 Listen and practice.

Bill	Hello?
Brandon	Hey, Bill. It's Brandon. Listen, do you want to see a movie tonight?
Bill	Tonight? I'm sorry. I can't.
Brandon	Oh, OK. Well, maybe some other time.

Melissa	Hello?
Brandon	Hi, Melissa. This is Brandon. Do you want to see a movie tonight?
Melissa	A movie? Sure. I'd love to.
Brandon	Great.

C 🎧 Listen to the expressions. Then practice the conversation again with the new expressions.

Declining an invitation

I'm sorry. I can't.	I'm afraid I can't.	I'm really sorry, but I can't.

Accepting an invitation

Sure. I'd love to.	Sounds good.	Yeah. That sounds great.

D **PAIR WORK** Practice the conversations again with the activities below.

get some ice cream	hang out	play video games	watch TV

A: Hello?

B: Hey, Bill. It's Brandon. Listen, do you want to get some ice cream tonight?

2 Listening I'd love to, but ...

A 🎧 Listen to four people invite their friends to do things tonight. Number the pictures from 1 to 4.

1

B 🎧 Listen again. Do the friends accept or decline the invitations? Check (✓) the correct answers.

1 ☑ accept   2 ☐ accept   3 ☐ accept   4 ☐ accept
  ☐ decline   ☐ decline   ☐ decline   ☐ decline

3 Speaking Do you want to hang out?

CLASS ACTIVITY "Call" your classmates and invite them to do something with you right now. Your classmates accept the invitations or decline them with excuses. Use the ideas below or your own ideas.

Possible things to do	Possible excuses	Responses to excuses
go out for coffee	I'm cooking dinner.	Oh, that's OK.
go to a party	I'm not feeling well.	Maybe next time.
see a movie	I'm eating lunch.	I'm sorry you can't make it.
go to the mall	I'm studying for an exam.	OK, I understand.
hang out	I'm doing my homework.	That's all right.
go shopping	I'm working late tonight.	No problem.

A: Hello?

B: Hi, it's me. Do you want to go to the mall?

A: I'm really sorry, but I can't. I'm not feeling well.

B: OK, I understand. Maybe next time.

I can accept or decline an invitation. ✓

C Planning a party

1 Vocabulary Party checklist

A 🎧 Match the things on the checklist and the pictures. Then listen and check your answers.

THINGS TO DO

1. ☑ bake a cake
2. ☐ buy a gift
3. ☐ choose the music
4. ☐ decorate the room
5. ☐ make a guest list
6. ☐ plan the menu
7. ☐ prepare the food
8. ☐ send invitations

B **PAIR WORK** When is a good time to do each thing in Part A? Discuss your ideas.

2 weeks before the party	2–3 days before the party	the morning of the party
1 week before the party	the day before the party	1 hour before the party

"A good time to make a guest list is two weeks before the party."

2 Conversation I can bake!

🎧 Listen and practice.

Andrea We have a lot of things to do for Eric's birthday party. Look, I made a checklist.

Mark Good idea. Who's going to help us?

Andrea Rosario. She's going to send the invitations.

Mark How is she going to send them?

Andrea By email.

Mark Good. That's easy. What are we going to buy for Eric?

Andrea Let's get him a sweater.

Mark Great. Who's going to bake the cake?

Andrea I'm going to bake it.

Mark Um, do you think that's a good idea?

Andrea Hey, I can bake!

Mark OK.

3 Grammar 🎧 *Wh-* questions with *be going to*; object pronouns

What are we going to buy **Eric**?	Let's get **him** a sweater.
Who's going to bake **the cake**?	Andrea's going to bake **it**.
How is she going to send **the invitations?**	She's going to send **them** by email.

Subject	I	you	he	she	it	we	they
Object	me	you	him	her	it	us	them

A Complete the conversation with the correct forms of *be going to*. Then practice with a partner.

A What time _____*are*_____ you ____*going to go*____ (go) to Eric's birthday party?

B _____ (go) to the party at 6:45.

A How _____ you _____ (get) there?

B My friend Jason _____ (drive). Do you want a ride?

A Um, sure, thanks! What _____ you _____ (do) after the party?

B Jason and I _____ (go) out. I think we _____ (see) a movie.

B Rewrite the sentences. Use object pronouns. Then compare with a partner.

1 He's not going to invite Mary. _____*He's not going to invite her.*_____

2 Let's call Bill and Ami again. _____

3 I'm going to see Eric tomorrow. _____

4 He's going to help Debbie and me. _____

5 We're going to buy the present tomorrow. _____

6 Call Rosario at 5:00. _____

C CLASS ACTIVITY Ask your classmates what they're going to do tonight. Answer with your own information.

4 Speaking Let's decide together.

A PAIR WORK Discuss the situations.

Your classmate Masao is in the hospital. He has nothing to do. What are you going to bring him?	You're planning your friend's birthday party. Where is it going to be? What are you going to eat and drink?	You want music for your teacher's birthday party. What songs are you going to play? How are you going to listen to them?

A: What are we going to bring to Masao?

B: Let's bring him a new video game.

A: That's a great idea. How about … ?

B GROUP WORK Share your ideas with another pair. Ask and answer questions for more information.

5 Keep talking!

Go to page 151 for more practice.

I can discuss and agree on plans. ✓

D Birthdays

1 Reading 🎧

A What was the last party you went to? What did you do at the party?

B Read the article. Which birthdays are special in each country?

NIGERIA
In Nigeria, the first, fifth, tenth, and fifteenth birthdays are very special. To celebrate these birthdays, people have big parties and invite up to 100 people. They eat "jollof rice." This is rice with tomatoes, red peppers, onions, and cassava, a kind of potato.

JAPAN
The third, fifth, and seventh birthdays are very important in Japan. Every year on November 15th, three-year-old boys and girls, five-year-old boys, and seven-year-old girls celebrate the *Shichi-go-san* (Seven-five-three) Festival. They usually wear traditional clothes and eat "thousand-year candy" for a long life.

BIRTHDAY TRADITIONS AROUND THE WORLD

ECUADOR
In Ecuador, a family has a big party when a girl turns 15 years old. The birthday girl wears a dress, and her father puts her first pair of high-heeled shoes on her. Then he dances with her. Fourteen other girls dance with fourteen other boys at the same time.

SOUTH KOREA
Parents in South Korea sometimes try to guess a child's future on his or her first birthday. They put the child in front of some objects, such as a book and a coin. They wait to see which object the child takes. For example, a book means the child is going to be a teacher. A coin means the child is going to have a lot of money.

C Read the article again. Answer the questions.

1   On special birthdays, what do Nigerian children eat?   *They eat "jollof rice."*

2   Who celebrates *Shichi-go-san*?   _____

3   Who dances with a 15-year-old Ecuadorian girl at her birthday party? _____

4   How do South Korean parents guess a child's future?   _____

D **PAIR WORK** How did you celebrate your last birthday? Tell your partner.

"I celebrated my last birthday with my friends. We ate out at a nice restaurant."

2 Listening Sweet 16

A 🎧 Listen to Amanda, a 16-year-old American girl, describe her "Sweet 16" birthday party. Check (✓) the true sentences.

1 ☑ Amanda's birthday is July 14th.

      She
2 ☐ ~~Her parents~~ made a guest list.

3 ☐ She sent the invitations.

4 ☐ She and her father decorated the room.

5 ☐ She had pizza, ice cream, and cake.

6 ☐ Forty of her friends came.

7 ☐ She got a gift from her parents.

8 ☐ She's going to have a party on her 18th birthday.

B 🎧 Listen again. Correct the false sentences.

3 Writing A thank-you note

A Think of a birthday gift (or any gift) you received. Answer the questions.

- What is the gift? _____
- Who is it from? _____
- Why did you get it? _____
- What do you like about it? _____

B Write a thank-you note for the gift. Use the model and your answers in Part A to help you.

C GROUP WORK Share your thank-you notes. Did any of you write about similar gifts?

> Dear Liz,
>
>   Thanks a lot for the birthday gift. I love the sweater. Blue and green are my favorite colors. Thank you for coming to my party!
>
>   Thanks again,
>   Sun-hee

4 Speaking How we celebrate

A GROUP WORK Discuss the ways people celebrate birthdays in your culture. Use the questions below and your own ideas.

- Which birthdays are very special?
- Do people celebrate with family, friends, or both?
- What do people eat and drink?
- What do people do?
- Do they give gifts? What kinds of gifts?
- How do you usually celebrate birthdays?

B GROUP WORK Tell your group how you are going to celebrate your next birthday. Are you going to do any of the things you discussed in Part A?

a birthday party in Mexico

I can describe birthday traditions in my culture. ✓

Wrap-up

1 Quick pair review

Lesson A Guess!

Say three dates when you are going to do something special. Can your partner
guess what you are going to do? Take turns. You have three minutes.

A: I'm going to do something special on June 17th.

B: Are you going to graduate?

A: Yes, I am!

Lesson B Do you remember?

Read the sentences. Write A (accepting an invitation), D (declining an invitation),
or E (making an excuse). You have one minute.

1 I'd love to. _____

2 I'm studying for an exam. _____

3 That sounds great. _____

4 I'm really sorry, but I can't. _____

5 I'm working late tonight. _____

6 I'm afraid I can't. _____

Lesson C Brainstorm!

Make a list of things you do to plan a party. How many do you know?
You have two minutes.

Lesson D Find out!

What are three activities both you and your partner do on your birthdays?
You have two minutes.

A: I eat cake on my birthday. Do you?

B: Yes, I eat cake, too.

2 In the real world

When is your birthday? Go online and find information in English about two important
events that happened that day. Then write about them.

- Where did the events happen?
- Who participated in the events?
- Why were the events important?

My Birthday

My birthday is December 17th. On this day in
1903, the Wright brothers flew an airplane for 12
seconds. This was important because …

Name circle

A **GROUP WORK** Stand in a circle. Go around the circle and say your first names. Repeat your classmates' names before you say your own name.

B **GROUP WORK** Go around the circle again. Repeat your classmates' full names.

A: My name is Eduardo Sanchez.

B: His name is Eduardo Sanchez. My name is Ming-mei Lee.

C: His name is Eduardo Sanchez. Her name is Ming-mei Lee. My name ...

Entertainment awards

Student A

PAIR WORK You and your partner have pictures of the same people, but some of the jobs and cities are different. Ask questions to find the differences. Circle them.

Jun Sasaki
Singer
Osaka

David Mason
Actor
London

Antonio Loren
Model
Rome

Maria Lopez
Actress
Los Angeles

Lucy Chen
Artist
Hong Kong

Alice Johnson
Musician
New York City

A: Is Antonio Loren a model in your picture?

B: Yes, he is.

A: OK. That's the same. Is he from Rome?

B: No, he's from Milan. That's different.

Keep talking!

Around the world

A Create a "new" identity. Write your new name and the country and city you are from.

Name:
Country:
City:

B GROUP WORK Interview four classmates. Complete the cards with their "new" identities.

Name:
Country:
City:

Name:
Country:
City:

Name:
Country:
City:

Name:
Country:
City:

A: Hi. What's your name?

B: Hi. My name is Sophie Manet.

A: Where are you from, Sophie?

B: I'm from France.

A: Oh, you're French. What city are you from?

B: I'm from Paris.

Keep talking!

Entertainment awards

Student B

PAIR WORK You and your partner have pictures of the same people, but some of the jobs and cities are different. Ask questions to find the differences. Circle them.

Jun Sasaki
Artist
Osaka

David Mason
Actor
Boston

Antonio Loren
Model
Milan

Maria Lopez
Singer
Los Angeles

Lucy Chen
Actress
Hong Kong

Alice Johnson
Musician
Chicago

A: Is Antonio Loren a model in your picture?

B: Yes, he is.

A: OK. That's the same. Is he from Rome?

B: No, he's from Milan. That's different.

Keep talking!

Family tree

A Draw your family tree. Include your family members, their names, and their ages.

My father, Cesar

My mother, Emilia

My brother, Cesar

Me, Roberto

My wife, Claudia

Our daughter, Isabel

Our son, Ivan

My Family Tree

B **PAIR WORK** Tell your partner about your family tree, but don't show it! Your partner draws it on another sheet of paper. Take turns.

A: My grandfather is George. He's 72 years old. My grandmother is Anna.

B: How do you spell "Anna"?

A: A-N-N-A.

B: OK, thanks.

A: She's 68. Their kids are ...

C **PAIR WORK** Compare your drawing with your partner's family tree. Are they the same?

Cleaning the closet

PAIR WORK Look at Dean and Lucy's closet. What things are in their closet?

A: What's that?

B: It's a dictionary. What's that?

A: It's a cell phone. Hey, what are these?

Keep talking!

What color?

Student A

A `PAIR WORK` You and your partner have pictures of the same people, but some of their clothes are different colors. Describe the clothing to find the differences. Circle them.

A: In my picture, Alice's coat is blue and white.

B: That's the same in mine. And her pants are gray.

A: In my picture, her pants are green. That's different.

B `PAIR WORK` Cover the picture. What is the same? Answer with the information you remember.

A: Alice's coat is blue and white.

B: Yes. And Ben's pants are …

What color?

Student B

A PAIR WORK You and your partner have pictures of the same people, but some of their clothes are different colors. Describe the clothing to find the differences. Circle them.

A: In my picture, Alice's coat is blue and white.

B: That's the same in mine. And her pants are gray.

A: In my picture, her pants are green. That's different.

B PAIR WORK Cover the picture. What is the same? Answer with the information you remember.

A: Alice's coat is blue and white.

B: Yes. And Ben's pants are ...

Keep talking!

Car, train, bus, or bicycle?

A Look at the ways people get to work in Los Angeles.

How people in Los Angeles get to work	
73%	drive alone
10%	drive with others
7%	take the bus, train, or subway
3%	walk
1%	ride a bicycle
5%	work from home

Note: % = percent

B **PAIR WORK** Guess the ways people get to work in Washington, D.C. Complete the chart with the numbers. Then check your answers on the bottom of page 134.

1%	4%	5%	6%	13%	32%	39%

How people in Washington, D.C. get to work	
_____ %	drive alone
_____ %	drive with others
_____ %	take the bus, train, or subway
_____ %	walk
_____ %	ride a bike
_____ %	other
_____ %	work from home

C **GROUP WORK** Guess the ways people get to work where *you* live. Rank them from 1 to 8.

_____ drive alone   _____ ride a bicycle   _____ take the bus, train, or subway   _____ walk

_____ drive with others   _____ take a taxi   _____ work from home   _____ other

A: I think number 1 is "take the bus, train, or subway."

B: I agree. I think number 2 is "drive alone."

Routines

A CLASS ACTIVITY Find classmates who do each thing. Write their names.

Find someone who …	Name	Find someone who …	Name
gets up before 6:00		sleeps a lot on weekends	
studies in the morning		walks to class	
takes a shower at night		has a red bike	
has coffee at home		reads on the bus	
reads every day		takes a bath in the morning	
goes to bed early		drives a sports car	
watches TV after midnight		doesn't cook	

take a shower

study on the bus

drive a sports car

A: *Do you get up before 6:00, Donna?*

B: *No, I don't. I get up at 6:30.*

A: *How about you, Michael? Do you get up before 6:00?*

C: *Yes, I do.*

B Share your information.

A: *Michael gets up before 6:00.*

B: *And Angela gets up before 6:00. David studies in the morning.*

Answers to Keep talking! Unit 4 Lesson A, Part B (page 133): 32% drive alone; 6% drive with others; 39% take the bus, train, or subway; 13% walk; 4% ride a bike; 5% work at home; 1% other

134   Keep talking!

On the computer

A Add two more questions about online activities to the chart.

Do you ever … ?	Name:
read people's blogs	
buy books online	
watch movies online	
search the internet in English	
write articles or blogs	
chat with friends online	
listen to podcasts	

search the internet in English

chat with friends online

buy books online

B **PAIR WORK** Interview your partner. Complete the chart with his or her answers. Use adverbs of frequency.

A: *Naoko, do you ever read people's blogs?*

B: *Oh, yes. I often do. Do you?*

A: *I hardly ever do.*

B: *Do you ever …*

C **PAIR WORK** Tell another classmate about your partner's answers.

A: *Naoko often reads people's blogs.*

B: *Sasha never does.*

Follow-up questions

A Add two more questions about each topic to the charts.

Sports and games	Questions	Name: _____
	Do you ever play sports?	
	What do you play?	
	Who do you play with?	

Shopping	Questions	Name: _____
	Do you ever go shopping?	
	Where do you shop?	
	What do you buy there?	

Getting around	Questions	Name: _____
	Do you ever take the bus?	
	Why do you take the bus?	
	When do you take it?	

B **CLASS ACTIVITY** Find a classmate who does each activity. Then ask the follow-up questions. Take notes.

A: Do you ever play sports, Samantha?

B: Yes, I sometimes do.

A: What do you play?

B: I play tennis.

C Share your information. What answers are popular in your class?

Keep talking!

Job details

A Look at the picture for two minutes. Try to remember the people's names, jobs, and other information.

B **PAIR WORK** Cover the picture. Ask the questions and answer with the information you remember.

- What does Ana do?
- Where does she work?
- Who does she work with?
- What does Paul do?
- How does Jane get to work?

- What does Luis do?
- Where does Mei-li work?
- What does she do?
- What company does Mitch work for?
- What does Carla do?

A: *What does Ana do?*

B: *I think she's a waitress.*

A: *Yes, I think so, too. Where does she work?*

C **PAIR WORK** Ask and answer two more questions about the picture.

Start to finish

GROUP WORK Play the game. Put a small object on *Start*. Toss a coin.

 Move 1 space.

Heads

 Move 2 spaces.

Tails

Read the question. Can you do what it says? Take turns.

Yes. → Move forward.   No. ← Move back.

Keep talking!

What's in your shopping basket?

A Choose seven items to put into your shopping basket. Circle them.

B **PAIR WORK** Find out what is in your partner's basket. Can you make the dishes below with the food in your baskets?

Stew
beef
carrots
noodles

Fruit smoothie
apples
bananas
milk

Spaghetti and meatballs
beef
cheese
pasta
tomatoes

A: I have beef and noodles. Do you have any carrots?

B: Yes, I do. We can make stew!

C **PAIR WORK** What else can you make with the food in your baskets?

How often do you eat standing up?

GROUP WORK Add two eating habits to the list. Then discuss how often you do each thing.

drink coffee in the morning

drink tea

eat alone

eat junk food in class

eat fast food for breakfast

eat on the street

eat standing up

(your own idea)

(your own idea)

A: Do you ever drink coffee in the morning?
B: Yes, I do.
C: How often do you drink coffee in the morning?
B: I drink coffee in the morning three times a week. How about you?

Keep talking!

What's missing?

Student A

A PAIR WORK You and your partner have pictures of the same neighborhood, but different places are missing. Ask questions to get the names. Write them.

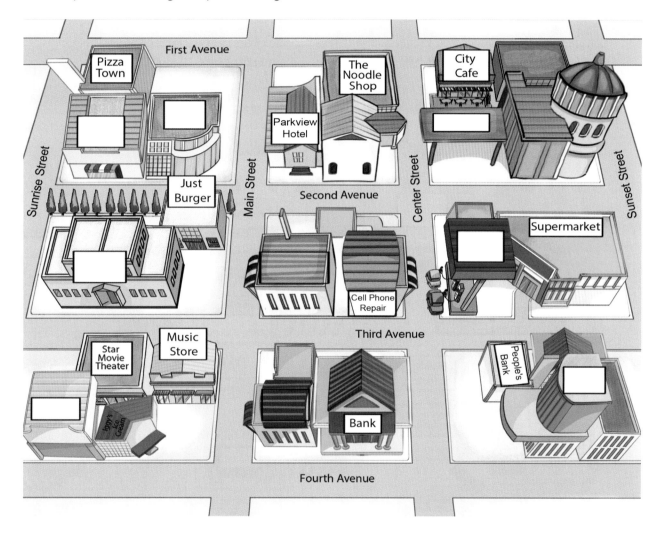

A: What's next to the supermarket?

B: The gas station.

B PAIR WORK Cover the picture. Tell your partner six things you remember.

A: The gas station is next to the supermarket.

B: That's right.

What's missing?

Student B

A **PAIR WORK** You and your partner have pictures of the same neighborhood, but different places are missing. Ask questions to get the names. Write them.

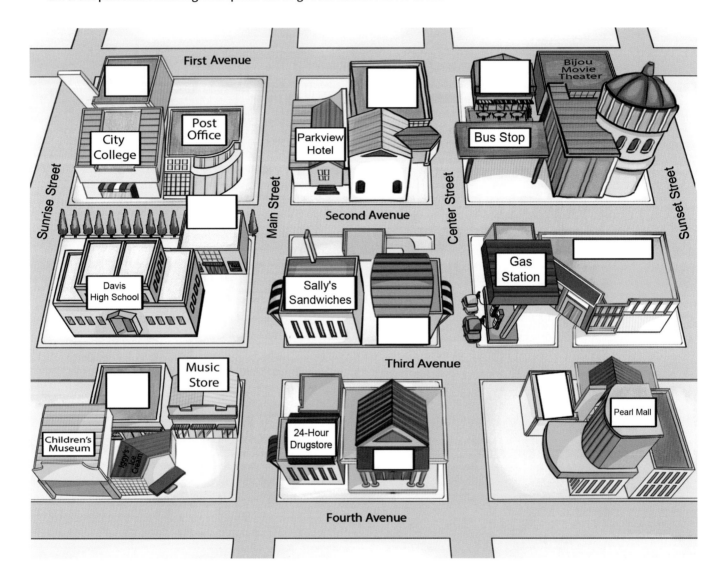

A: What's across from the post office?

B: Parkview Hotel.

B **PAIR WORK** Cover the picture. Tell your partner six things you remember.

A: Parkview Hotel is across from the post office.

B: That's right.

Keep talking!

An unusual zoo

PAIR WORK What's wrong at this zoo? Make ten sentences about the people, animals, and other things in the zoo. Use *There is …* , *There are …* , and prepositions of location.

"There's a bear in the car."

Keep talking!

Neighbors

A **PAIR WORK** Look through the windows. What are the people doing? Discuss your ideas.

A: I think the man is doing his homework. What do you think?

B: I think he's writing a letter. He's sitting, too.

B **PAIR WORK** What are the people actually doing? Go to page 153 to check your answers.

Keep talking!

Who is it?

A Write three sentences about what you're doing these days on three pieces of paper.
Don't write your name!

I'm tutoring a student.   I'm taking tennis lessons.   I'm not studying every night!

B **GROUP WORK** Put your papers on the table. Take one paper and read the sentences. Your group
guesses the name. Take turns.

A: This person is tutoring a student.

B: Is it Juliana?

C: No, it's not me!

D: Is it Kate?

C **GROUP WORK** Discuss the activities you're doing these days. Ask and answer questions
for more information.

A: Who are you tutoring these days, Ken?

B: I'm tutoring a friend of mine. His name is Luke.

C: Are you tutoring him in English?

B: No, I'm not. I'm tutoring him in Japanese.

Picture story

A PAIR WORK Look at the pictures of David and Emma Salas. What did they do last weekend? Use the verbs to discuss your ideas.

clean	fix	play	stay out	watch
dance	paint	shop for	study	

A: David and Emma cleaned the house.

B: Emma fixed her bike.

B PAIR WORK Cover the pictures. What did David and Emma do last weekend? Answer with the information you remember.

Keep talking!

Memories

GROUP WORK Make five true sentences about your past activities with the phrases below. Your group asks three questions about each sentence for more information. Take turns.

Yesterday	Last night	Last weekend	Last month	Last year
I drank …	I ate …	I saw …	I bought …	I went …
I got up …	I went to bed …	I had …	I read …	I met …
I did …	I slept …	I drove …	I made …	I took …

A: Last night, I ate soup for dinner.

B: Did you eat in a restaurant?

A: No, I didn't. I ate at home.

C: Did you make the soup?

A: No, I didn't. My son made it.

D: Did you … ?

School trips

A PAIR WORK Add three more questions about school or work trips to the list. Then interview your partner. Take notes.

1 What was your favorite school or work trip?

_____

2 How old were you?

_____

3 How was the trip?

_____

4 Was there anything bad about the trip?

_____

5 Did you take a bus there?

_____

6 Were you there all day?

_____

7 Did you buy anything?

_____

8 _____

_____

9 _____

_____

10 _____

B PAIR WORK Tell another classmate about your partner's answers.

"Michi's favorite school trip was to a cookie factory. She was ten years old. The trip was ..."

Keep talking!

What a vacation!

A Look at the items from Adriana's vacation. Write five questions and answers about her vacation.

1. Where did Adriana go on vacation?
   New York City.

2. What kind of music did she hear?
   Jazz music.

B GROUP WORK Cover the picture. Ask your questions. How many correct answers did your group get?

Keep talking!

This weekend

A Make eight true sentences about your plans with the phrases below.

My plans		
I'm going to I'm not going to	dress up eat out go to a concert go to bed late go to the mall go window-shopping hang out study watch a movie work	tonight this evening tomorrow this weekend next Monday next Friday

dress up

go to a concert

go window-shopping

B PAIR WORK Tell your partner about your plans. Ask and answer questions for more information.

A: I'm going to go to bed late tonight.

B: Are you going to watch a movie tonight?

A: No, I'm not. I'm going to study.

Keep talking!

Party planners

A GROUP WORK Plan an end-of-class party. Take notes.

Date of party	Time of party	Place of party

Food and drink	Decorations	Music

A: When are we going to have our party?

B: Let's have it after class on Friday at 8:00.

C: OK. Now, where are we going to have it?

D: Let's have it here at the school.

B CLASS ACTIVITY **Share your ideas. Ask and answer questions for more information.**

A: We're going to have our party on Friday at 8:00.

B: It's going to be here at our school.

C: Which room is the party going to be in?

C CLASS ACTIVITY **Vote for your favorite plan.**

Irregular verbs

Base form	Simple past
be	was, were
become	became
build	built
buy	bought
can	could
choose	chose
come	came
do	did
draw	drew
drink	drank
drive	drove
eat	ate
fall	fell
feel	felt
fly	flew
get	got
give	gave
go	went
hang	hung
have	had
hear	heard
hold	held
know	knew
leave	left

Base form	Simple past
lose	lost
make	made
meet	met
pay	paid
read	read
ride	rode
run	ran
say	said
see	saw
sell	sold
send	sent
sing	sang
sit	sat
sleep	slept
speak	spoke
spend	spent
stand	stood
swim	swam
take	took
teach	taught
think	thought
wear	wore
win	won
write	wrote

Answer Key

Unit 9 Lesson A (page 144)
Keep Talking! Neighbors

Credits

The authors and publishers acknowledge the following sources of copyright material and are grateful for the permissions granted. While every effort has been made, it has not always been possible to identify the sources of all the material used, or to trace all copyright holders. If any omissions are brought to our notice, we will be happy to include the appropriate acknowledgements on reprinting and in the next update to the digital edition, as applicable.

Photography

All below images are sourced from Getty Images.

U1: Dougal Waters/DigitalVision; Idea Images/The Image Bank; drbimages/E+; Shannon Fagan/Blend Images; Alys Tomlinson/Cultura; kali9/E+; Gary John Norman/Blend Images; Vincent Sandoval/Getty Images Entertainment; Michael Tran/FilmMagic; Jason Merritt/Getty Images Entertainment; Kevin Winter/WireImage; Noam Galai/FilmMagic; PeopleImages/DigitalVision; ©Christa Van Den Heuvel; Jason Merritt/Getty Images Entertainment; Manuel Blondeau - Corbis/AOP Press/Corbis Sport; ©GV Cruz; Jim Spellman/WireImage; ©Everett Collection; ©Scott Gries; ©Kevin Mazur; Victor Chavez/WireImage; Focus on Sport; ©Jon Kopaloff; Kevin Mazur/Getty Images Entertainment; **U2:** miniature/DigitalVision Vectors; ©Patricio Robles Gil; Caiaimage/Tom Merton/OJO+; JohnnyGreig/E+; Ronnie Kaufman/Larry Hirshowitz/Blend Images; Sami Sert/E+; Geber86/Vetta; Rob Lewine; PhotoAlto/Frederic Cirou/PhotoAlto Agency RF Collections; manaemedia/iStock/Getty Images Plus; ake1150sb/iStock/Getty Images Plus; **U3:** Harvey Lloyd/Photolibrary; Stewart Cohen/Photolibrary; H. Armstrong Roberts/ClassicStock/Archive Photos; Tim Brown/Stone; BeholdingEye/iStock/Getty Images Plus; koya79/iStock/Getty Images Plus; ©iStock; ©Hemera; ©E+; SKYRENDER/iStock/Getty Images Plus; Sean Justice/Photonica; gielmichal/iStock/Getty Images Plus; DorlingKindersley; Jerome Gorin/PhotoAlto; nipastock/iStock/Getty Images Plus; Yagi Studio/DigitalVision; maroke/iStock/Getty Images Plus; NYS444/iStock/Getty Images Plus; Eri Morita/Photodisc; Franco Origlia/Getty Images Entertainment; Images Plus; Dorling Kindersley; istock; Nikolai Sorokin; E+; ©istock; ©caimacanul/iStock/Getty Images Plus; Imagesource; creativesunday2016/iStock/Getty Images Plus; ©istock; **U4:** Radius Images/Radius Images/Getty Images Plus; Garden Photo World/David C Phillips/Canopy; Brent Winebrenner/Lonely Planet Images; artpipi/iStock/Getty Images Plus; microgen/iStock/Getty Images Plus; miljko/E+; Fuse/Corbis; Sam Edwards/Caiaimage; Wavebreakmedia/iStock; Indeed; PeopleImages/E+; ©photodisc; ©Hero Images; ©Hemera; ©Istock; Yongyuan Dai/Stone; **U5:** iPandastudio/iStock/Getty Images Plus; monkeybusinessimages/iStock/Getty Images Plus; pictafolio/iStock/Getty Images Plus; OnstOn/iStock/Getty Images Plus; KeremYucel/iStock/Getty Images Plus; Jane_Kelly/iStock/Getty Images Plus; Madmaxer/iStock/Getty Images Plus; Geert Weggen/Aurora Photos; Westend61; JGI/Jamie Grill/Blend Images; Tetra Images; Photoplotnikov/iStock; MicrovOne/iStock; Jupiterimages/Photolibrary; Creative Crop/DigitalVision; Grzegorz Wozniak/EyeEm; rasslava/iStock/Getty Images Plus; UmbertoPantalone/iStock/Getty Images Plus; mattjeacock/iStock/Getty Images Plus; 3alexd/iStock/Getty Images Plus; valentinrussanov/E+; Morsa Images/Iconica; Boogich/E+; ©Perry Mastrovito; Jean-Pierre Lescourret/Lonely Planet Images; Sam Edwards/OJO Images; golibo/iStock/Getty Images Plus; imagedepotpro/E+; ultramarinfoto/E+; Jeffrey Coolidge/Photodisc; Thomas-Soellner/iStock/Getty Images Plus; Spencer Platt/Getty Images News; Vimvertigo/iStock/Getty Images Plus; Thearon W. Henderson/Getty Images Sport; Akimasa Harada/Moment Open; Tara Moore/DigitalVision; dlerick/iStock; **U6:** JohnnyGreig/E+; RUBEN RAMOS/iStock Editorial/Getty Images Plus; Digital Vision; Joerg Lehmann/StockFood Creative; PeopleImages/E+; ljubaphoto/iStock/Getty Images Plus; Andersen Ross/Cultura; Jenny Acheson/Iconica; ©Workbook Stock; hjalmeida/iStock/Getty Images Plus; Wavebreak Media Ltd/Getty Images Plus; DAJ; Jean Luc Morales/The Image Bank; Sven Hansche/EyeEm; LIU JIN/AFP; Todd Pearson/The Image Bank; PRImageFactory/iStock/Getty Images Plus; EricLatt/iStock Editorial; Owen Franken/Photolibrary; **U7:** ahirao_photo/iStock/Getty Images Plus; twomeows/Moment; Angela Schintu/EyeEm; Jason England/EyeEm; MARIAMARTAGIMENEZ/iStock/Getty Images Plus; ©istock; ©E+/Getty Images; Wavebreakmedia/iStock/Getty Images Plus; MIXA; EricVega/iStock/Getty Images Plus; ©Hemera; Eric Audras/ONOKY; guruXOOX/iStock/Getty Images Plus; yulkapopkova/iStock/Getty Images Plus; Stockbyte; Zakharova_Natalia/iStock/Getty Images Plus; Photodisc; asbe/iStock/Getty Images Plus; Piotr Krzeslak/iStock/Getty Images Plus; rez-art/iStock/Getty Images Plus; ©Image Source; Claudia Totir/Moment; Roger Stowell/Photolibrary; SUNGSU HAN/iStock/Getty Images Plus; MargoeEdwards/iStock/Getty Images Plus; PhotoAlto/Laurence Mouton/PhotoAlto Agency RF Collections; Jupiterimages/PHOTOS.com/Getty Images Plus; Kevin Mazur/WireImage; **U8:** Ken Welsh/Photolibrary; guruXOOX/iStock/Getty Images Plus; Education Images/Universal Images Group; Jeff Greenberg/Universal Images Group; Richard Cummins/Lonely Planet Images; Glow Wellness/Glow; Alija/E+; csfotoimages/iStock Editorial/Getty Images Plus; Barry Winiker/Photolibrary; JoeMcBride; Fuse/Corbis; fotog; Wolfgang Kaehler/Getty Images; Judy Bellah/Lonely Planet Images; Tim Bieber/Photodisc; John Leyba/The Denver Post; John Leyba/The Denver Post; Chad Baker/Jason Reed/Ryan McVay/Photodisc; Erik Tham/Corbis Documentary; DragonImages/iStock/Getty Images Plus; PhotoTalk/iStock/Getty Images Plus; Thomas Barwick/Taxi; PRImageFactory/iStock/Getty Images Plus; PhotoAlto/Laurence Mouton/Getty Images; **U9:** Westend61; jacoblund/iStock/Getty Images Plus; Robert Deutschman/Robert Deutschman; Wavebreakmedia/iStock/Getty Images Plus; Tom Merton/Caiaimage; Wavebreakmedia/iStock/Getty Images Plus; Andersen, Ross; Alija/E+; Eric Audras/ONOKY; PeopleImages/E+; JGI/Tom Grill/Blend Images; fizkes/iStock/Getty Images Plus; Image Source/Getty Images; Dougal Waters/DigitalVision; monkeybusinessimages/iStock/Getty Images Plus; drbimages/E+; Car Culture/Car Culture ® Collection; Qvasimodo/iStock/Getty Images Plus; John Harper/Corbis Documentary; Parichat Boon-Ek/EyeEm; Peter Bannan/Moment; VStock LLC/Tanya Constantine; Martin Paul/Photolibrary; Ryan McVay/The Image Bank; Caiaimage/Paul Bradbury; Jose Luis Pelaez Inc/MNPhotoStudios/Blend

Images; **U10:** Andreas Kuehn/DigitalVision; Hoxton/Tom Merton/Hoxton; Photos.com/PhotoObjects.net; lewkmiller/iStock/Getty Images Plus; Wavebreakmedia/iStock/Getty Images Plus; Elke Meitzel/Cultura; Neil Beckerman; Thomas Barwick/Taxi; Ryan McVay/The Image Bank; Huntstock/Getty Images; Lambert/Archive Photos; DMEPhotography/iStock/Getty Images Plus; Aneese/iStock Editorial/Getty Images Plus; Andrew Olney/Getty Images; jarenwicklund/iStock/Getty Images Plus; bowdenimages/iStock/Getty Images Plus; MGP; Gregory Costanzo/; flashfilm/Taxi Japan; Stockbyte/; Plume Creative; FluxFactory/E+; Erik Isakson/Blend Images/Getty Images Plus; BLOOMimage; **U11:** Jupiterimages/Stockbyte PhotoAlto/Ale Ventura/PhotoAlto Agency RF Collections; andresr/iStock/Getty Images Plus; PRImageFactory/iStock/Getty Images Plus; Caiaimage/Paul Bradbury; BLOOMimage; JeanUrsula/E+; Image Source; robbie jack/Corbis Entertainment; istock/Getty Images; MangoStar_Studio/iStock/Getty Images Plus; andrej_k/iStock/Getty Images Plus; Manuel-F-O/iStock/Getty Images Plus; Andersen Ross/Blend Images; Jon Feingersh/Stone; ©Otto Stadler/; visualspace/iStock/Getty Images Plus; Westend61; Hector Vivas/Jam Media/LatinContent Editorial; Thomas Barwick/Taxi; Ferdaus Shamim/WireImage; Glow Images, Inc/Glow; Ariel Skelley/DigitalVision; Rohan Van Twest; VisitBritain/Britain on View; PhotoAlto/Ale Ventura/PhotoAlto Agency RF Collections; **U12:** Sam Edwards/OJO Images; Burke/Triolo Productions/The Image Bank; Stephanie Keith/Getty Images News; xavierarnau/E+; Jose Luis Pelaez Inc/Blend Images; Steve Fitchett/Photographer's Choice; Christian Kober/AWL Images; PhotoAlto/Laurence Mouton/Getty Images; Jose Luis Pelaez Inc/MNPhotoStudios/Blend Images; Westend61; PhotoAlto/Ale Ventura/PhotoAlto Agency RF Collections; fotografixx/iStock/Getty Images Plus; Photo and Co/The Image Bank; Luis Alvarez/Taxi; Amy Eckert/Taxi; Michael Powell/Photolibrary/Getty Images; YOSHIKAZU TSUNO/AFP; kali9/iStock; Ann Ronan Pictures/Print Collector/Hulton Archive; **End Matter:** VisionsofAmerica/Joe Sohm/Photodisc; Jeffrey Greenberg/Universal Images Group; David Harrigan/Canopy; hedgehog94/iStock/Getty Images Plus; Car Culture/Car Culture ® Collection; JerryPDX/iStock/Getty Images Plus; Radius Images/Getty Images Plus; pop_jop/DigitalVision Vectors; 4x6/iStock/Getty Images Plus; RichLegg/iStock/Getty Images Plus; baona/iStock/Getty Images Plus; alikemalkarasu/E+; Hemera Technologies/PhotoObjects.net/Getty Images Plus; Rawpixel/iStock/Getty Images Plus; ©Daniel Grill/Tetra; ©E+; ©imagesource; ©Tetra Images; ©istock; ©Greg Elms/StockFood Creative; ©PhotoAlto; ©Stockbyte; anna1311/iStock/Getty Images Plus; nicmifsud/iStock; McIninch/iStock/Getty Images Plus; vgajic/E+; Mikael Vaisanen/Corbis; iPandastudio/iStock/Getty Images Plus; Jonathan Knowles/The Image Bank; Wavebreakmedia/iStock/Getty Images Plus; Clerkenwell/Vetta; kali9/E+; Image Source RF/DreamPictures; Fraser Hall/robertharding; JGI/Jamie Grill/Blend Images; PeopleImages/E+; Neil Beckerman/Getty Images; Hero Images.

Front Cover by Sergio Mendoza Hochmann/Moment; Betsie Van der Meer/DigitalVision; andresr/E+.
Back Cover by Monty Rakusen/Cultura.
The following images are sourced from other libraries:
U1: ©Allstar Picture Library/Alamy; **U2:** ©Joana Lopes/Shutterstock; ©RubberBall/Alamy; Alamy; ©Derek Trask/Alamy; **U3:** ©Media Bakery; ©Shutterstock; Frank Veronsky; Oleksiy Maksymenko/Alamy; Squared Studios/Ocean/Corbis; ©slon1971/Shutterstock; ©Helene Rogers/Alamy; **U4:** ©Liu Xiaoyang/Alamy; ©Patrick Eden/Alamy; ©David Gee/Alamy; © Frank Veronsky; Shutterstock; Media Bakery; Pushish Images/Shutterstock; **U5:** © Frank Veronsky; ©Robert Clayton/Alamy; ©DavidSanger/Alamy; ©Alex Segre/Alamy; **U6:** ©Golden Pixels/Alamy; ©Pinnacle Pictures/Media Bakery; **U7:** ©Evlakhov Valeriy/Shutterstock; ©Adrianna Williams/Corbis; ©Frank Veronsky; ©ampFotoStudio/Shutterstock; ©Bon Appetit/Alamy; **U8:** Frank Veronsky; Iain Masteron/Alamy; Tomas Abad/Alamy; Frans Lemmens/Alamy; **U9:** Blend Images/Alamy; Ted Foxx/Alamy; Ian Shaw/Alamy; Andrea Matone/Alamy; JeffreyIsaacGreenberg/Alamy; ACE STOCK LIMITED/Alamy; Vehbi Koca/Alamy; **U11:** Gavin Hellier/Alamy; Idealink Photography/Alamy; tomas del amo/Alamy; JL Images/Alamy; picturesbyrob/Alamy; Frank Veronsky; Ditty_about_summer/Shutterstock; IM_photo/Shutterstock; Neale Cousland/Shutterstock; **U12:** dam eastland/Alamy; dbimages/Alamy; Frank Veronsky; **End Matter:** ©Judith Collins/Alamy; ©Hugh Threlfall/Alamy; ©Holger Burmeister/Alamy; ©David Lee/Alamy; imageBROKER/Alamy; dbimages/Alamy.

Illustration

Front Matter: Kim Johnson; John Goodwin; **U1:** Kim Johnson; QBS Learning; **U2:** Peter Ellis; QBS Learning; Dani Geremia/Beehive Illustration; **U3:** Dani Geremia/Beehive Illustration; Peter Ellis; Rob Schuster; Kim Johnson; QBS Learning; **U4:** QBS Learning; **U6:** Dani Geremia/Beehive Illustration; QBS Learning; **U8:** QBS Learning; **U9:** Szilvia Szakall/Beehive Illustration; Garry Parsons; Peter Ellis; QBS Learning; **U10–12:** QBS Learning; **End Matter:** Dani Geremia/Beehive Illustration; QBS Learning.

Dani Geremia/Beehive Illustration pp20, 26, 56, 129, 137; Szilvia Szakall/Beehive Illustration pp86, QBS Learning pp5, 16, 29, 30, 32, 33, 35, 40, 57, 59, 60, 76, 78, 79, 81, 93, 96, 99, 109, 120, 125, 126, 127, 130, 131, 132, 135,138, 141, 142, 143, 144, 146, 147, 149

Art direction, book design, and layout services: QBS Learning
Audio production: CityVox, NYC and John Marshall Media
Video production: Steadman Productions